WEIRD FACTS ABOUT FISHING

Strange, Astonishing & Hilarious

Jeff Morrison

OVER TIME BOOKS

The Publisher: OverTime Books
OverTime Books is an imprint of Éditions de la Montagne Verte

Library and Archives Canada Cataloguing in Publication

Morrison, Jeff, 1967–
    Weird facts about fishing: I fish therefore I am / Jeff Morrison.

Includes bibliographical references.

ISBN 978-1-897277-42-3

    1. Fishing—Miscellanea. I. Title.

SH443.M68 2010   799.1   C2009-906811-7

Project Director: J. Alexander Poulton
Editor: Heather MacDonald
Cover Image: Courtesy of iStockPhoto:©seanfboggs/SFB Photographics Inc./iStockPhoto.com

We acknowledge the financial support of the Government of Canada through the Book Publishing Industry Development Program (BPIDP) for our publishing activities.

 Canadian   Patrimoine
Heritage   canadien

PC: 5

Contents

Dedication

I dedicate this book to my father, Rathwell Morrison, without whom my love and appreciation for the Great Outdoors may never have been realized. Thanks, Dad, for all the fabulous fishing trips over the years—here's to enjoying many more to come.

–Jeff Morrison

Acknowledgments

I would like to thank the many fine writers before me who felt it worthy to document the copious facets of one of North America's favorite pastimes. Thanks also to the Outdoor Writers of Canada (OWC) Association for being on top of market opportunities as always, and to OverTime Books for giving me the chance to leave my imprint on an already successful *Weird Facts* book series. A special thanks also to my editor Heather MacDonald for all her hard work. And last, but certainly not least, a huge note of appreciation to my wife, Cheryl, for supporting me on this project every step of the way, and for typing until her fingers were numb. Or at least that's what she kept telling me.

Introduction

Those who put aside time in their busy lives to participate in one of the oldest recreational activities on earth do so not merely for enjoyment, but also because of a burning passion for the sport. Fishing is an activity that varies greatly among participants in North America. There are literally hundreds of different techniques and styles dating back to the early days when our forefathers strung up 10-foot long bamboo poles with old Dacron line. But, as varied and changing as the sport is among its avid anglers, fishing does hold a few key similarities, as I quickly discovered while researching this book. True fishing fanatics are as crazy as loons and all seem to share one common interest: a deep love and respect for the great outdoors. That can be said of Larry Toben, who jigs for cod off the Grand Banks of Newfoundland; Frank Green, who casts a fly for salmon in Prince Rupert; Pierre Lemieux, pursuing brook trout in Quebec's Magantic region; or John Stevens, trolling for striped bass off the New England coast. They all possess a love for the sport and an unparalleled commitment.

For me, it started around the age of four when my grandfather would take me to Caribou Lake after school to learn his trick for catching a pail full of sunfish and perch in no time flat. You see, I grew up in a busy country inn in Quebec's Laurentian Mountains, and my parents were often too busy running the business to take me out, so my "Gonka" was there to pick up the slack, God bless his heart. But on days off, my dad would always make a point of taking me to our camp in the mountains to share with me his great love of nature and, of course, his favorite pastime, which just happened to be sportfishing. The many positive attributes and excitement of fishing I picked up in those early days are still near and dear to my heart today, nearly 40 years later.

The common thread of passion and commitment shared by different angers around the globe, however, does carry certain adverse effects—the by-products, you might say, of a sport enjoyed by millions. The folks most committed to the passions in their lives, it seems, often have weird things happen to them along the way. Perhaps it is the adrenaline rush they get when pursuing an activity they love that clouds their judgment. I'm not sure, but strange and abnormal are certainly part of the intrigue of sportfishing today, as I believe has been the case throughout history. Those who sought finned creatures with hook and line 200 years ago were every bit as crazy as the diehard professional bass anglers we see today. Let's face it; fishing enthusiasts are a quirky lot. They are proud, slightly disturbed and love nothing more than recounting a tale or two with anyone who will listen.

Throughout this book, we see how an underlying drive that brings people out on the water can oftentimes produce a comical situation and the odd far-fetched big fish story along the way. *Weird Facts about Fishing* takes a historical look at various fish species and delves into the minds and hearts of anglers from across North America. We see what makes these people tick, and occasionally what drives them nuts! You are treated to a smattering of impressive statistics and more tall fish tales than you can shake a stick at. The movie *Jaws* may have whipped people into a sub-aquatic fear frenzy at local beaches back in the 1970s, but today there are even more ominous water creatures lurking underwater, every bit as scary as that old mechanical shark. Come take a bird's eye journey through a sport that contributes $125 billion each year to the

U.S. economy alone. It's a sport that draws family and friends to summer cottages on the weekend, one that bonds brothers, sisters, mothers, fathers and close friends, drawing them even closer. It's a fact: fishing is about love, passion, fear, intrigue and a whole lot more. As my father once told me: fishing is a sport where you don't necessarily need to be crazy to be good at it, but it certainly does help!

The timing of this *Weird Facts* series couldn't have been better when you look at the world climate. As we muddle our way through a global recession, learn to deal with two wars in the Middle East and an economy in turmoil, the safe haven created in an activity like sportfishing should not be overlooked. I am happy to say there's a trend observed in North America over the last several years that shows an increase in recreational activities like hunting and fishing.

As wacky as it can be sometimes, fishing is one activity that brings great joy and excitement to anyone who has ever experienced it. Take it from a 42-year-old man who still gets heart palpitations from the tug of a 15-inch brook trout on the end of his line. At that special moment when angler and fish connect through thin monofilament, all the woes of the world seem to magically disappear. And there is no better time than the present to get involved in the sport, no greater way to clear your head and learn to laugh at yourself, instead of others, for a change.

Fishing is an easy and inexpensive therapy and there is nothing else like it in the world to make you smile. The sport has many facets and factions—each one more mysterious than the last. Sit back and enjoy a look at one of weirdest and most wonderful activities known to man.

Chapter One

A Face Only a Mother Could Love

In this chapter we delve into the mysterious and misunderstood side of some of the lesser-known fish species of North America. We will take a gander at some of the less prestigious and more esthetically challenged specimens found in our waters today. There are some weird and wacky creatures swimming in our lakes and rivers, and very few people are even aware of it. We will take a peek at some exotic and alien fish species that now call our local waters their home. Some of the strangest things are going on under the surface, and if we knew half of it most of us would probably never go swimming again. Some odd fish are hatchery produced—as a hybrid of two existing strains or species—while others are accidental introductions into non-native waters such as is the case with the Asian carp, sea lamprey and northern snakehead. Exotic fish species are those creatures that exist in areas outside North America

but somehow—often through human-engineering mishaps—now live in our waters. Other fish species, such as the bowfin and lake sturgeon are actual throwbacks to a prehistoric time with hundreds of years of history behind them. What do all these prehistoric creatures, exotics and other strange and wonderful fish have in common? Well, let's just say they certainly wouldn't win any beauty or popularity contests!

Sea Lamprey

Ask anyone around the Great Lakes what a sea lamprey is, and they will usually cringe. These predatory and parasitic eel-like creatures have wreaked great havoc on native fish in the Great

Lakes in recent years. The sea lamprey, to be honest, is basically a large bloodsucker that latches onto any unsuspecting host, usually large game fish found in the Great Lakes. They, like the American eel, are catadromous reproducers in that they breed in the Atlantic Ocean and travel inward through freshwater streams and rivers to feed. The sea lamprey undergoes several life stages, gradually developing an inborn need to suck blood and body fluids from a host using its razor-sharp teeth and a grasping tongue. They often leave their host fish dead or severely injured. In ongoing studies done in Lake Huron, as many as 20 percent of the fish sampled had lampreys attached to them, showed healing wounds or had scars from lampreys. It has been estimated by researchers that the sea lamprey, over the course of its life, will kill an average of 18.5 pounds of fish. Approximately three pounds of blood is required to raise a sea lamprey from metamorphosis up to sexual maturity.

So what is being done to control this parasitic intruder, you ask? Throughout the Great Lakes, efforts are being made to control its increase. Through extensive studies, dating back to the 1970s, the Great Lakes Fishery Commission and the U.S. Fish and Wildlife Service have discovered that sea lampreys are most vulnerable at three specific stages in their development. The larval stage is when they are most vulnerable to attack since the population is sedentary, and any sort of control measure would have an immediate effect. The metamorphosis stage is another time where the proposed method of destruction of the newly metamorphosed sea lampreys would have a good effect in preventing them from migrating. Another stage when they are vulnerable and, open for destruction is when they are concentrated in either migratory or sedentary groups and may be eradicated during these two phases.

One effective method of destroying this strange and destructive parasite is through the construction of low overhead dams on waterways to prevent their migration because lamprey are unable to leap higher than two feet. The most commonly used chemical control is called PFM and it is a type of lampricide. This chemical is used under strict control to kill larval lamprey without causing harm to other fish species. Bayer 73 is another form of lampricide that can be used in combination with PFM. Unfortunately, it is also toxic to some other fish species, so the struggle to control this parasite continues in and around the Great Lakes. It is anticipated that that one day the sea lamprey will be eradicated altogether.

Did you know?

Flying fish actually glide on wind currents sometimes up to 20 feet above the surface of the water.

Bowfin

The bowfin is one mysterious and crazy-looking fish—an ancestor of the Jurassic and Cretaceous periods and one of the few freshwater fish to be considered a contemporary of the dinosaurs. The bowfin is quite distinctive with an extremely long dorsal fin, cylindrical body and ice age-like head. They are found in eastern North America in various rivers and ox-bow lakes (a lake that has been formed out of a pre-existing curve of a river). The bowfin is also distinct in that it must rise to the surface and gulp air to re-inflate its swim bladder. They can grow up to three feet in length and weigh upward of 15 to 20 pounds. The bowfin also has a distinctive spot near its caudal fin or tail. It is believed this eye spot at the tail serves as a distraction for predators because, if you look at it quickly, one cannot tell which end of the fish is the head, thus allowing them to escape danger. Besides being mysterious-looking compared to other freshwater fish in eastern North America, the bowfin is actually quite similar in behavior to other piscivorous, or fish-eating, fish. They can be caught on artificial lures and provide great sport for anglers who are lucky enough to catch them. The bowfin is a powerful fish and can be extremely dangerous, as they often try to bite when being removed from a hook. The roe or eggs from the bowfin can be made into bowfin caviar, which is a delicacy for some, considered to be much like the highly sought after caviar of sturgeon. The bowfin, on sheer looks alone, is another weird fact of fishing today.

Some of the best fishing is done not in water but in print.

–Sparse Grey Hackle, *"Murder" Fishless Days*

Longnose Gar

The longnose gar is another freaky throwback to prehistoric days, which can still be found in localized populations across North America. The gar is a regular inhabitant of the Great Lakes-St. Lawrence region, and although the fish are difficult to hook because of their long, serrated bill, anglers in the know with the right equipment have learned to be quite successful at catching them. Even some renowned fishing guides on

the Ottawa and St. Lawrence Rivers will specifically target this rare species. Because of their legendary fighting ability, most of the gar captured
by anglers are subsequently released as they are
not seen as providing great table fare. Since they
are built like tanks with plated armor on the outside
of their bodies to protect them from predators,
they have few enemies. I can vividly recall the
impressive strength these fish possess from a gar
I caught many years ago at my friend's cottage on
Six Mile Lake near Georgian Bay. It was only
about a 6-pound gar but I can remember dis-
tinctly the way it felt as it shook each time I tried
to remove the hook, easily powering its way free
of my grasp. This powerhouse could not be contained with just one hand. You don't see that
kind of strength in northern pike or even muskie
of the same size. Although it may have been the
one and only gar I've ever caught, the feel of its
armor-like scales and muscular, streamlined
body was something I will never forget.

Alligator Gar

Throughout the United States, from the Florida
panhandle to the Mississippi drainage to the
Ohio and Missouri Rivers and over to Mexico, you
will find the alligator gar—the largest and most
fearsome member of the gar family. The alligator
gar is considered by many to be the ultimate

trophy sports fish in North America because they have been reported up to 350 pounds and 10 feet in length. They are a very large fish with a broader, bulkier build than the long nose gar and, as the name implies, look very much like an alligator with a fish's tail. Alligator gar, besides being quite impressive and intimidating because of their size, are not known to be aggressive with humans; however, they do have a voracious appetite and will eat just about anything that they can fit in their mouths. Numerous videos and exciting big fish stories exist on the Internet about the alligator gar. They have become the stuff of legends and more than a few nightmares too, I would imagine.

The Northern Snakehead

The northern snakehead is another odd fish that is native to the Yangtze River in China where they survive in large numbers. However, as with many other accidental introductions into North American waters, they can also be a scary sight and create substantial damage. The northern snakehead story in the United States dates back to the turn of the new millennium when a restaurant owner from New York City reportedly ordered some snakeheads to make soup for his restaurant. Well, that's when all the trouble started. The northern snakehead, you see, is a very peculiar fish in not only its looks but in its ability to breathe air. These critters can live for several days out of water and in China are often packaged and shipped live as they will remain fresh for longer, providing a fresher meal.

It is believed that the New York restaurant owner received his snakeheads for soup but found them too cute to eat, so later decided to put them in his aquarium instead. As the story goes, his two snakeheads quickly consumed all the "feeder fish" the restaurant owner offered them, and in no time became too large for the aquarium. It is believed the man then released them into a pond behind the house where these native-Chinese fish had their run of all the local pan fish in the lake, which they made short work of devouring. As time went on, the snakeheads reproduced and eventually found their way into other nearby water systems. They have reportedly even been caught by anglers in Maryland and turned into the Department of Natural Resources for examination.

Because of their ability to breathe air and the fact that they are extremely resilient and have such a ravenous appetite, the northern snakehead is a real concern to local waters. Some people call them the "Jaws" of the new millennium. They are yet another example of an exotic fish species accidentally released into non-native waters.

Within a year, it was discovered that the snakeheads had been found in six other U.S. states.
In 2008 President George W. Bush announced
trade and import bans on 28 snakehead species,
in an attempt to prevent any further spreading. The
northern snakehead is another weird and wonderful fact in the world of fishing today, though
probably weirder than they are wonderful.

IT'S A FACT

In Seattle, Washington, it is legal for goldfish to
ride the city buses in bowls, but only if they keep still.

More Than Just Caviar

The sturgeon is one the weirdest and most
mysterious fish known to man. They are strange
and unique for several reasons. One reason is
their size. Sturgeon is actually the name given to
more than 20 different species of large bottom-
feeding anadromous fish. They are found in
waters across North America; however, they usually dwell in rivers and feed in quiet estuaries
connected to the ocean. Sturgeon can range in
size from two to 12 feet in length depending on the
subspecies and region they are found in. Some goli-
ath Beluga sturgeon from the Caspian Sea have

been reported in the 18 to 20 foot (5.5 to 6 metres) range, and tipped the scales at over 4000 pounds (1800 kilos). The most common lake sturgeon is found in many rivers and lakes across the country and occasionally caught by anglers who target this fragile species. They are highly prized for their caviar—most notably the beluga caviar—as well as for having other unique characteristics that make them weird. They are often referred to as the Methuselahs of the deep because of their ability to live up to 100 years in some cases. And since they often do not reach sexual maturity until they are 25 years old, the stability of sturgeon populations has always been tentative.

Most sturgeon species across North America are in various stages of peril. They are either on the decline or listed as threatened or endangered species. Since they are anadromous, by and large, they spend much of the time in fresh waters living and feeding in our North American rivers and then migrate great distances to find suitable areas to deposit their eggs. Migration barriers such as dams that do not allow the sturgeon to move freely in the rivers will eventually cause their downfall. They are distinctive in their appearance as well. Not only are they huge, but they are prehistoric in looks as well. Often called a living fossil, every sturgeon species has four barbels (whiskers), underneath its mouth, used for feeding in the benthic, or bottom, regions. They are toothless and docile, and we are encouraged to release these living giants if we ever catch one. Yes, they are one freaky fish and perhaps one of the most fragile species in existence as well.

Asian Invasion

The dreaded Asian carp is, without a doubt, this century's greatest natural resource blunder. The ravenous fish species from Asia—capable of growing to over 100 pounds—has already destroyed much of the Mississippi and Missouri River watersheds, spreading into much of the Midwest including 15 U.S. states. The Asian carp is an ancestor and direct descendant of the common carp we all know and have, well, come to despise. The common carp was an introduction to North American waters that make few of us very proud. They are large, bloated specimens of a fish that have already exploded throughout much of the Great Lakes-St. Lawrence System and into most of continental North America.

The common carp has out-competed native fish species at every turn and is one of this continent's examples of how a non-native exotic fish can run amok in non-native waters. And if you think they're bad, the Asian carp is a totally new intruder altogether. The Asian carp has trampled through the Mississippi River Watershed like a herd of longhorn cattle, in such a way that they now make up 90 percent of the fish population in that region. They are prolific and vicious, eating anything in sight including vast amounts of forage food and other game fish and have even become a danger to boaters. They must be bad if they have garnered the attention of Congress in the United States with a new bi-partisan bill that will ban the import of any new Asian carp-related species.

In a speech, U.S. Senator Carl Levin described the fish as being "like a bull in a China shop" and said they are hazardous to boaters, cause damage to property and cause injuries. These menacing fish were originally introduced in the United States as an aquaculture tool and a fish for sewage treatment facilities. Voracious eaters, they were used in the 1970s in states such as Louisiana as a biological control on fish farms. But as with many other projects with good intentions, things went terribly awry, and flooding allowed these aggressive killers to escape the ponds and enter into the Mississippi River watershed. In the last 15 years, they have completely devastated the region's aquatic habitat.

The Asian carp is an invader, the likes of which we have never seen before, and should this aggressive non-native species ever make its way into the Great Lakes, there would be no stopping them.

The only thing keeping them from getting into the system is an electric power dam in Chicago that, should it ever malfunction, the carp could utilize to gain access to hundreds and hundreds of miles of cold northern waters habitat in which they could live quite nicely. Asian carp are not only weird, they are downright nasty!

Over the years, whenever I've felt that little twinkle in the hairs on the back of my neck, as I encounter an original thought or observation in a fishing book, I've turned the corner of the page down.

–Arnold Gingrich, *The Fishing in Print—A Guided Tour Through Five Centuries of Angling Literature*

See-Through Fish, What Next?

At a time when fish species are swimming ram-pant out of control, while other plants and animals seem to be creeping their way onto the threatened or endangered species list, it is encouraging when we discover the presence of a friendly new fish species. The fact that they may not be beautiful should have no bearing on it. Take for example the see-through barreleye fish, a species that, thanks to the work of the Monterey Bay Research Institute, has single-handedly solved a 50-year old mystery. The see-through barreleye fish is aptly named for its eyes that are barrel-shaped and unique in the way that they face upward to detect the silhouette of prey from above. The most unique and mysterious part of the barreleye is the front portion of this fish from its snout to the back of its head and pectoral fins is completely see-through. Much like those novelty telephones back in the 1980s, the barreleye has translucent skin on part of its body that fully exposes the inner work-ings of this crazy-looking specimen.

Another unique fact of the see-through barrel-eye is the area of the ocean in which they are found. They were discovered in the Meso-Pelagic Zone of the Pacific Ocean, which ranges from 1300 to 8200 feet below the surface. They are also unique in the way that they are pelagic spawners, which is to say that the fish's eggs and sperm are released in a large mass at the same depth of water—buoyant and subsequently fertilized at unbelievable depths in the ocean. Though they may not be the Brad Pitts or Angelina Jolies of the fish world, they are an encouraging fact of existence because they cause no apparent environmental damage and appear rather friendly—a welcomed change in a society of turmoil.

New Antarctic Creature

Another welcome visitor to modern day life is the eelpout, a species discovered recently during a British research expedition in the Indian Ocean between Africa and Antarctica. The specimen retrieved by researchers measured 1.35 feet in length and was captured at an unbelievable depth of 2.8 miles below the surface. The eelpout was an encouraging find during this 2006 expedition and British researchers have hopes that it may be just the tip of the iceberg. They have also commented that, although the eelpout is no looker, we should keep in mind that beauty really is individual.

Lies, Lies and More Lies

In the fishing world, as in other facets of society, you will find urban legends, hoaxes and other general falsehoods. Some hoaxes found in the fishing world, as weird as they sound, are every bit as far fetched as your average fish story.

Perhaps the oddest fish hoax in recent history was the supposed deep sea creatures washed up by the 2004 Indian Ocean tsunami. The media, the Internet and word of mouth spread the story like wildfire. Images of prehistoric fish species were everywhere with captions like "Indian Ocean Tsunami Stirs Up Creatures from the Deep," with attached graphic images of several strange and scary-looking beasts. It is unfortunate that hoaxes are a reality today especially when centered on a catastrophic world event such as the 2004 tsunami. But as we have witnessed, nothing is really sacred anymore.

As quickly as the tsunami fish story circulated, fortunately, so too did the presence of debunkers ready to shoot the story down. Something smelled, well, fishy! Marine biologists contributed to uncovering this story as a hoax by confirming that, although the fish in the photos were indeed bona fide deep-sea creatures, they had nothing to do with the Indian Ocean tsunami. The images were really pirated from a 2003 expedition carried out in the Tasman Sea by the Australian and New Zealand governments. The study was entitled "The Norfanz Voyage" and was a research project carried out from May to June 2003 to look at the region's biodiversity. These photographs evidently appealed to someone's vivid imagination, and the tsunami fish story took on a life of its own.

As long as there are weird fish in the world, we will have weird fish stories that are occasionally untrue.

Mother Nature is not fooled by technological fixes.

–Robert Behnke, *In Praise of Wild Trout*

Chapter Two

Ambassadors of the Sport

Sportfishing, let me tell you, has seen its fair share of colorful characters over the years. There have been a number of important ambassadors to the sport, all of whom have contributed, in one way or another, to the popularity of fishing today. Thanks to greatly expanded media coverage—including radio, television, the Internet and copious print media—sportfishing has reached each and every one of us in North America, in some way. A tip of the hat goes out to those brave mavericks of the industry for demonstrating various facets of the sport, and showing us that although it is a strange pastime on occasion, it also has great benefits. These well-known North American personalities have contributed far more to sportfishing than even they probably realize. For me, back in my formative years, it was guys like Al Lindner from the American Midwest who helped teach me about

the ways of the muskellunge, and later my passion
unfolded with Bob Izumi, my Canadian hero, on
television each and every week. Bob Izumi's *Real
Fishing Show* was a breakthrough for Canadian
television at the time and has remained a fixture
ever since. To these faithful fishing warriors and
many more, I salute you! Many of us here in the
outdoor field owe our livelihoods, our careers
and of course a greatly fostered interest in the
world's number one pastime.

Bob Izumi

What can you say about Canada's number one
ambassador and best-known angler? What can
you say about a guy who, not unlike many of us,
started from humble beginnings with a passion
for rod and reel? Bob grew up in a family of
seven. His parents raised their family in the
southwestern Ontario town of Blenheim. Bob's
father, Joe, was also instrumental in the very
first Canadian Bass Tournament and exposed Bob
and his brother Wayne to a sport that would
become a big part of their lives. Later on at a family
picnic, as the story goes and after Bob and Wayne
had already teamed up to win many a fishing tournament, someone suggested the idea of a fishing
show. Back in the early 1980s, fishing television
shows were somewhat of a rarity. Perhaps it was
destiny for the man to become Canada's first full-
time fishing professional in 1979; here we are

over 25 years later and Bob Izumi's *Real Fishing Show* is still going strong. Bob also developed his own company called Izumi Outdoors Inc. and along with his brother, Wayne, continues his vision of providing avid anglers with the information they need. Izumi Outdoors is all about educating and entertaining. It boasts a television production department, a magazine department, a radio show and also maintains a popular website. Izumi Outdoors has become a brand unto itself and taken on a life of its own, if you will. Izumi is not only a knowledgeable ambassador of the sport; he is also Canada's most successful tournament angler, a prolific outdoor writer, a conservationist and a seminar speaker with many years of experience behind him.

As of today, the *Real Fishing Show* and *Real Fishing Radio* are the longest-running television and radio series of their kind in Canada and Izumi continues to build on his reputation. Part of what makes Bob a colorful character is not just what he has done for this sport in Canada, but also for the man he is. He is approachable, possesses a certain youthful charm and exudes passion for the sport of fishing like no one else. This you can tell by watching his show, listening to his seminars or reading one of his books. Thanks Bob, for all you have done; you are an inspiration to all of us.

What about Bob?

Here are just a few little-known facts about Canada's king of fishing: Bob Izumi was born on May 2, 1958 in Chatham, Ontario. He won his first fishing derby at the age of eight and was only 20 years old when he became Canada's first full-time fishing professional. In 1998, he founded "Fishing Forever," a non-profit organization committed to conserving and enhancing Ontario waters and has remained the organization's chairman ever since. Bob is the only three-time winner of the Canadian Open Bass Tournament, and in 1995, he became Canada's only triple crown winner, which is to say that he won the Canadian Open, the G.M. Pro Bass Classic Championship as well as the G.M. Pro Bass Angler of the Year Award. He has authored three books, is an award-winning journalist with the Outdoor Writers of Canada and has co-hosted the *Real Fishing Show* for the past 20 years. What more can you say!

CONRAD VOSS BARK was the first BBC
Parliamentary Correspondent and for many
years served as Angling Correspondent to the
London Times. He lives in Devon, where his wife,

Anne, runs the famous Arundell Arms—but he
has fished with passion throughout the world.

–Nick Lyons, *The Quotable Fisherman*

"Big Jim" McLaughlin

"Big Jim" McLaughlin, or simply "Big Jim" to all his devotees, has been another Canadian icon over the last 25 years. Starting off his career as an avid tournament angler and winner of two CFT Canadian Classics, Canada's premier tournament series, McLaughlin has won an incredible number of other events including 28 tournament wins. He is the founder of the fishing publication *Just Fishing*, which is now in its 15th year of production and caters to the needs of Canadian and American anglers, and he was the host of *The Ultimate Fishing Show* before becoming a fishing show and seminar aficionado. The big guy is a featured emcee throughout the country each year, sharing his knowledge and gift for the sport, always with a big smile. He is a local celebrity in the Ottawa region with a heart as big as the man himself, and I'm proud to call him a friend. He has recently survived a battle with prostate cancer, throughout which he continued to do seminars and to offer tips to anglers across the country. He often travels over 100 days per year and promotes his *Just Fishing* magazine, a company that has become a family affair for Big Jim. He's an inspiration to anglers and more than willing to share a few secret tips on catching more fish, as well as his special take on conservation— something he prides himself on and has lived his life by.

ROBERT BECHNKE is our great trout biologist—the arbiter and authority on technical matters. Between reading Bob's work and that of Bill Willers, you'll know enough to "think like a trout," if that's what you really want to do.

–Nick Lyons, *The Quotable Fisherman*

Dave Mercer

Dave Mercer is another important Canadian personality. Mercer was just your typical Ontario boy who grew up with a passion and zeal for angling until he was 13, when he entered his first fishing tournament and won a quick $400. The idea of combining his favorite activity into a moneymaking venture was an interesting prospect for young Dave. By the time he hit his late teens, he was already hooked on the sport and starting to develop his own fishing tackle. The Hawg-Craw was a lure Dave created himself and peddled to local stores with hopes of turning his pastime into a career.

By the time he graduated from school he wanted to fish full time and approached a small local television network with the idea of 30 60-second fishing tip spots, and they went for it. Dave Mercer's *Sixty Second Fishing Reel* was an instant hit with over 80,000 viewers each week.

Dave had found a way of sharing his love of the sport with many viewers. His show was later named *Dave Mercer's Facts of Fishing* and became a regular series, reaching many more viewers. Soon Mercer released his own DVD fishing series. He even created a charity called "Dave Mercer's Casting for a Cure" to benefit the Canadian Cancer Society. He is a man that lives and breathes the sport, spending over 250 days on the water each year filming his shows and expanding his impressive DVD collection. The important thing about Dave, much like other ambassadors, is he has a lot to say. He balances his passion with a touch of humor and sensibility and is simply fanatic for the sport. As Mercer would say, "It's all fun and games until someone loses a fish."

ARNOLD GINGRICH used to get up at 4 AM, fish the Joe Jefferson Club ponds in all seasons, take the bus to New York City and practice the

*violin at Wurlitzer, and then arrive at his office
at* Esquire *magazine before 7:30. When I was
editing his* Joys of Trout, *he frequently called
me that early. Once he fell asleep at lunch—but
picked up the conversation without missing
a beat. A great man—and a great lover of
fly fishing.*

–Nick Lyons, *The Quotable Fisherman*

Italo Labignan

Italo Labignan is a graduate of my old alma mater, Sir Sanford Fleming School of Natural Resources, as a student of fishing and wildlife biology. Following SSFC, Italo worked with the Ontario Ministry of Natural Resources as a fisheries manager and pursued his interest in the outdoors and angling. Italo, eager for a career in natural resources, began working as an outdoor writer and a promoter of freshwater fishing in Canada. By the mid 1980s he had developed a good reputation as a highly knowledgeable conservationist and seminar speaker throughout the country. In 1985, Italo developed a concept of a new, more conservation-minded fishing series, which was the first of its kind in Canada. *The Canadian Sportfishing Show* was born and soon became a number one television series across the country. By the early 1990s, Italo's company was the largest outdoor communications company in Canada and had to its credit several published books, a travel division and a continuing television series, which has made Italo a household name. Today, he continues to be an important part of our fishing heritage and *The Canadian Sportfishing Show* continues with Italo at the helm, a man who has shown that a career in natural resource management is a possibility, a man who has faced adversity and many challenges. It's great to see folks like Mr. Labignan find a way to combine their passion and a career. Italo Labignan, in my opinion, is a true ambassador of the sport.

IT'S A FACT

In Liverpool, England, it is illegal for a woman to be topless in public unless she is a clerk in a tropical fish store.

Darryl Choronzey (Cronzy)

Darryl Choronzey was born in southern Ontario and spent his early years in the Port Colborne and Burlington area. He has become the backbone of the Canadian fishing industry and is often referred to as the "common person's fisherman." Unlike some of the other well-known personalities,

Cronzy, as he is known to his fans, is not a regular tournament angler but more of an enjoyment master and educator. His father and uncles taught him the sport he grew to love, and he soon became a well-known outdoor writer in his early days, writing for such publications as the *Globe and Mail*, the *Toronto Sun* and various magazines. Cronzy was also the editor and publisher of *Ontario Fisherman* magazine. For 15 years, it was the magazine of choice for serious anglers and Cronzy put his heart and soul into the publication for as long as it was around. He was a huge proponent of getting more people out on the water and stood by various causes including the reintroduction of Chinook salmon back into Georgian Bay, which is today considered one of the finest salmon fisheries in all of Canada. Today, Cronzy still hosts the *Going Fishing* television series, a series dedicated to the everyday angler. Thanks Darryl, for your many years of hard work and heartfelt commitment to sportfishing in Canada.

ERNEST HEMINGWAY. No writer has spawned more imitations or more commentary. I fished his Fox River, the prototype for his

*"Big Two-Hearted River," several years ago
and caught barely a fish.*

–Nick Lyons, *The Quotable Fisherman*

Patrick Campeau

Patrick Campeau is Canada's leading francophone fisherman. He is a full-time professional angler, outdoor writer and educator of the outdoors in the province of Quebec. He is another fine ambassador of the sport to the francophone community and has his fair share of tournament accomplishments, as well. According to a survey in *Outdoor Canada* magazine, Patrick Campeau is one of the Canadians with the most influence in the fishing industry over the past 30 years. He has qualified 44 times in the top 10 in the Professional Tournament Series and five times in the Canadian Open. He is a contributor to 16 magazines and newspapers and does a daily radio broadcast for more than 75 radio stations. In 2000 he won the coveted Pro Bass Champion and is the official host of several cottage and sportsmen shows. In 2008, Campeau became the spokesperson for the Fête de la Pêche for the province of Quebec, and in 2007 he was bestowed an honorary award from the Canadian Sportfishing Industry Association for his involvement and dedication to the sport. Patrick Campeau is one successful fisherman and a leader to francophone anglers throughout the country.

Did you know?

When an octopus gets angry, it shoots a stream of black "ink."

Al & Ron Lindner

Al and Ron Lindner have revolutionized fishing media in the United States since founding the In-Fisherman Company in 1975. The Brainerd, Minnesota, brothers, who lived and breathed the sport, became a true angling dynasty and built a company with annual revenues of over $10 million. Al and Ron Lindner started In-Fisherman, and it later became the nation's largest fishing multi-media communication company. In-Fisherman television was established in 1979 and was hosted by Al Lindner and reached nearly one million households. It aired every weekend. *In-Fisherman* magazine was published eight times per year and had more than a quarter of a million subscribers. The Lindners then launched *In-Fisherman Radio* in 1979, which now has over 800 affiliate stations across the Continental United States. Along the way, In-Fisherman has produced numerous videos, how-tos, books, instructional manuals and much more. The Lindner brothers were number one in the United States, and up until 1998, when they sold their company to a New York publishing company, they were the sole owners of the In-Fisherman Empire. Ron Lindner retired and Al stayed on with In-Fisherman until May 2002, when he left as host of the television series to start his own new TV shows called *Lindner's Angling Edge* and the *Fishing Edge* television series. In 1982 Al Lindner became a born-again Christian and wanted to take his new television series in an all-new direction to include a message of Christianity.

The Lindner brothers were also the creative forces behind the Lindner fishing tackle industry in the 1970s and the famous Lindy tackle in 1973, which was sold off before they began their media empire. The "Lindy Rig" is still available on the market today and remains a popular set-up for catching walleye. I owe a personal debt of thanks to Al Lindner for providing my early education on muskie, when I was a teenager and knew very little about muskie "hunting." Back in the early 1980s when I developed an interest in pursuing the elusive muskellunge, there was little training material available on this exciting sportfish. The Lindners' *Muskie Hunting* video series was crucial to my early days of muskie fishing. The Lindners were famous, not only for sharing their love of the sport, but also for crafting a more scientific approach to angling. They examined seasonal changes, lake and river structural patterns and taught that when it comes to fishing, knowledge is power. The Lindners' educated and scientific approach to the sport was partially responsible for my interest in fish and wildlife management today.

Babe Winkelman

Babe Winkelman became a household name on U.S. television 25 years ago. Winkelman is known as a guru of sportfishing and a world-class angler in his own right. The man is downright enthusiastic, whether he is working at his desk or on the water. He is prolific, too, frequently appearing in magazine and newspaper articles, broadcast segments and many major publications. As a presenter, Babe is every bit as inspirational as any of the best motivational speakers. Like the Lindners, Winkelman is from the Midwest, where he spent his early years fishing at this parents' cabin in Northern Minnesota. He began fishing competitively in the 1970s, and he even co-founded the Minnesota Bass Federation where he served as president for many years. He co-founded the Masters Walleye Circuit or the MWC where he emceed for numerous years and where he fished competitively for walleye, bass, muskie and other species.

Winkelman is known for being one of the most versatile anglers in the world and blessed with natural skills that few of us have ever seen, but his achievements have not gone to his head in any way. He still takes the time to fish with friends and family and shares his vast knowledge with anyone who will listen. He is probably best known for his walleye catching prowess on the lakes in and around Minnesota and the Midwest. In the early days, through his TV show *Outdoor Secrets*, Babe educated his viewers on conservation issues showing the merits of fishing and hunting on a weekly basis. As Babe put it so perfectly, "Fishing is not just a sport for men. It is for people, for families. There is an intimacy in the outdoors that you just can't get other places. I love to go fishing with family and friends as much as my schedule allows."

It is men like Babe Winkelman, another great ambassador of the fishing world, that keep this sport so vibrant.

Bill Dance

For all you southerners out there, there is Bill Dance—avid fisherman and the host of the *Bill Dance Outdoors Fishing Show*. Dance was raised in Lynchburg, Tennessee, and although his father had plans that he would be a doctor, all that changed after Bill was involved in a serious motorcycle accident in the 1960s. Dance began to focus on competitive bass tournaments, and one of his sponsors suggested that he start his own television show. For anyone who has ever watched Bill Dance on TV, he is about as entertaining and colorful as any host I've ever seen. His southern boyish charm has won over viewers from across North America, and Bill strives to produce the most real and honest look at our country's favorite sport.

Dance is a member of the International Game Fish Association's Hall of Fame and a three-time Bass Angler of the Year. In 1978, Dance was awarded the Congressional National Water Safety Award, and he joined the National Freshwater Hall of Fame in 1986. Bill began producing his fishing show with an ABC affiliate in Memphis in 1968, and his signature look of sunglasses and a Tennessee Volunteers baseball cap became a symbol to the hard-working everyday anglers of North America. *The Bill Dance Fishing Blooper Video* is perhaps the funniest fishing segment I have ever seen. Dance shows outtakes from his television series including true comical blunders. In one segment Bill falls out of the boat, and in another scene, snakes are raining down on him from trees above. In yet another clip, he's seen closing the tailboard of his pickup on a couple of fishing rods. There are so many other comical outtakes where the man simply shines and is doing so many of the things we have all done on occasion. We need more light-hearted men like Bill Dance, a man who is one more proud fact of fishing and a great ambassador of the sport.

Roland Martin

Famous Florida resident Roland Martin has created his fair share of waves in the fishing world over the past 25 years. Martin is not only a fine ambassador, but is considered by many to be the world's greatest angler, honing his skills on the Bassmasters Tour in the United States. Sporting his trademark bleach-blonde hair and dark Florida tan, Martin smiles from ear to ear, whether he is doing interviews or sharing the latest bass fishing techniques on his fishing show. In his career, Roland Martin has had a whopping 19 tournament wins, nearly 100 top 10 finishes, nine Angler of the Year titles and has also set a record for the most second place wins of any angler. On the Bass Tour, his career earnings had already exceeded $1 million by 2004, and he was the first professional bass fisherman to be inducted into all three halls of fame: the IGFA Hall of Fame, the Freshwater Fishing Hall of Fame and the

Professional Bass Fishing Hall of Fame. Martin is an ambassador for the sport, not just because of his angling achievements; he is also a fabulous promoter of various products and lures and has popularized what bass anglers called pattern-style fishing. Much like the Lindners did for muskie and walleye, Roland Martin has done wonders for the bass industry. He has preached both the pursuit of the American dream and the merits of conservation for over 25 years, and he has left his mark across North America as one of the most positive influences sportfishing could ask for.

*A.J. McClane's towering Encyclopaedia and his
many articles in* Field & Stream *and elsewhere
established him as the most knowledgeable
angler-writer of our time.*

–Nick Lyons, *The Quotable Fisherman*

Angelo and Reno Viola

For all those avid Canadian anglers out there, the mere mention of the Viola brothers or the *Fish'n Canada* television show will instantly bring back memories. Back in 1983, Angelo and Reno opened up one of the largest outdoor stores in the country at the time, Barklay's. Only Basspro in the United States was as big in its day. Barklay's was a store for the avid angler and hunter; it was at the time that the Violas also created Pro Bass and were instrumental in the tournament fishing series in Ontario. Pro Bass was the series where a lot of famous anglers got their start.

The Violas were a typical Ontario family and held a strong interest in fishing tactics and techniques and started their *Fishing Canada* empire in 1986, when the first season of the show aired across the country on CBC. It remains on the air today and is as popular as ever. *Fishing Canada* has seen its fair share of staff members, including Pete Bowman and Mike Miller, who travel the country in search of the biggest and most fearsome freshwater fish. The TV show has retained its reputation as being truly Canadian and strives to feature the greatest destinations Canada has to offer. After over 20 years on the show, Reno Viola decided to step down and retire, which caught many people off guard. Reno's retirement came as a bit of a shock, but there is no doubt that his contribution to the *Fishing Canada* legendary series was enormous. On top of the regular television show, the guys still do regular weekly television programs and maintain an active website with blogs, online videos and a whole lot more. Thanks to the Viola brothers for providing years of fishing entertainment on Canadian television and portraying the sport in the best possible light.

Frank Edgar

Not all of fishing's ambassadors are just anglers. When thinking about companies that have contributed greatly to make this sport the most popular in the world, Lucky Strike instantly comes to mind. Lucky Strike was the brainchild of one Frank Edgar, a tool and die maker in the 1920s. Edgar returned home during the Great Depression in the 1929 to Peterborough, Ontario, where he spent hours working on his wooden fishing plugs. His first fishing lures were, believe it or not, carved out of broom handles. By 1931, Edgar was commissioned to make 10,000 of these handmade plugs and, after getting a $75 loan to expand his business, he purchased a shipment of cedar and hired two boys to cut lumber for him. At the time, Frank Edgar did not have a name for his special fishing lure and decided to hold a contest. The name Lucky Strike was chosen. Edgar's sales continued, and he expanded his garage workshop in Peterborough.

A second factory was added in 1944 in Cobourg, Ontario, and the production of his lures really took off. Who would have thought an old wooden plug with Frank Edgar's name on it would become so important in fishing today? Lucky Strike has become one of the largest tackle companies in the world and continues in the family tradition started by Frank Edgar and his wife, Elsie. After Frank passed away, Bill Edgar, Frank's son, took over as the general manager of Lucky Strike. Today, Bill's daughter, Mary, and her husband, Kim Rhodes, have assumed the role of general managers of Lucky Strike. I hope as long as there is fishing, there will be a Lucky Strike lure at the local bait shop and tackle store. To look back on the history behind this company makes me smile. Bill Edgar is retired today but still has some input into the Lucky Strike operation, a company his father founded and one in which he surely feels great pride.

Steve Raymond's books are always among the most thoughtful writings about fly fishing. He has also been one of our sturdiest and most demanding critics.

–Nick Lyons, *The Quotable Fisherman*

George Breckenridge

Brecks fishing tackle has a long and prestigious history behind it. Founder George Breckenridge, who settled in Quebec's Eastern Townships, spent much of his younger years fishing in a plethora of lakes and rivers in the region. In 1947, Breckenridge started his company with his wife, Maude, where they manufactured and marketed lures right from their home. As his first love was fishing, what better way, he thought, to forge a career than by selling something so close to his heart. In 1964, his son David took over the company and they continued to expand with the manufacturing of their famous Williams Wobbler—one of the premier fishing spoons on the market today. Brecks has since added many other fabulous lures along the way. As a pioneer and one of the oldest family-run tackle businesses in North America, George Breckenridge's tackle was always entirely manufactured in Sherbooke, Quebec. The stamping, ringing, forging and packaging of the lures have always been done from one central location. Brecks has also produced many other great lures in its series, including the whitefish, the trophy, the bully, the ice jig and many more.

The concept of a family owned and operated business serving as a fine ambassador of the sport of fishing is not something new. We have witnessed the same with other famous Canadian manufacturers, such as Lucky Strike, and with the Heddon Company in the United States. According to Breckenridge, the true test of a lure is the test of time, and there have been thousands of lures that have come and gone over the past century. The key components used in the Brecks manufacturing facility are what made the difference. Brecks has always used real gold, silver and brass—all materials that stand the test of time. Since the acquisition of Mooselook in 2003, the Brecks manufacturing company has expanded its worldwide recognition with the production of a full line of Williams and Mooselook Wobblers, and continue their tradition today. Although George Breckenridge passed away 15 years ago at the age of 94, his legacy lives on as perhaps one of the most important personalities on the Canadian fishing scene.

James Heddon

The name James Heddon is synonymous with artificial fishing lures. The company that bears his name was founded in 1902 and originally manufactured handmade wooden lures out of the family kitchen in Dowagiac, Michigan. The fishing lures that James Heddon created in those early days were later mass produced by the Heddon Lure Company. By 1910, Heddon had sales connections in Canada and a factory in Michigan. By 1950, the Heddon Company was churning out an incredible 12,000 lures a day. There has not been a single person in the history of fishing who has created such a stir and paved the way for so many other lure aficionados. The Heddon lure changed fishing forever, as did the quiet, humble man James, who started off as a beekeeper in Michigan but who had great aspirations of a change for the fishing industry. Not only did he revolutionize the industry, which was soon to become a multi-billion dollar per year industry, but he also created an interest in the collection of antique lures.

The Heddon lure company has changed hands many times since the early days when James sat in his kitchen carving, but some of the noteworthy dates when Heddon created his masterpieces are well documented. Before the 1900s, Heddon's original tackle was made from broomsticks, whittled away by the man himself. By 1902, the first manufactured fishing lures were created at a time when James and his son William worked together, and William moved to Florida to test his new plugs as the company began to grow. By 1932, the first plastic fishing lures were introduced under the Heddon name followed by a whole series of famous fishing lures such as the Dowagiac Minnow, the Heddon Frog, the Woodpecker, the Musky Surfacer, the Spindiver and the Flipper. Other famous lures are the River Runt and the Artistic Minnow. Heddon was a colorful character and an ambassador of the sport, not simply for the way he created these masterpieces, but for the legacy he left behind, paving the way for an abundance of lure enthusiasts, fishing collectors and vintage tackle organizations.

The Canadian Sportfishing Industry Association (CSIA)

The CSIA is an interest group established to ensure the stability of the $6.7 billion a year recreational fishing industry. The CSIA recognized the importance of this industry and sought a fine balance in Canada. Its members include a network of retail operations such as Canadian Tire, independent retailers, distributors and manufacturers such as Zebco, Shimano, Pure Fishing and Normark, and many of the larger media operations in Canada. The CSIA is important and reaches out to other interest groups such as the Canadian National Sportfishing Foundation (CNSF) and deals with recreational fishing and fisheries management. The important activity of National Fishing Week—Canada's largest fishing promotion—combines the strengths of government, media and other outdoor volunteer organizations. Since fishing is an integral activity for many Canadian families, the organization seeks to keep these activities a tradition and hopes to expose Canadians of all ages to the merits of fishing. Through its sister organization, the Canadian

National Sportfishing Foundation, there is an aggressive promotion program to make fishing more accessible and to maintain angling as a heritage activity. Money from the sale of fishing licenses provides a large chunk of revenue to manage fish populations across the country and the CNSF is not alone in its efforts to get fellow Canadians out on the water. There are many other organizations that deal directly with the CSIA in promoting fishing as a viable activity. Some of the issues that the organization has dealt with in recent years are the historic Atlantic Salmon Restoration Project; Forest, Fish and Wildlife on the Firing Line; and their work on having the lead sinker ban withdrawn. The CSIA is a fabulous organization that works in the best interest of fishermen and women with the common goal of conserving and ensuring the future of this great sport.

Kevin VanDam

Kevin VanDam is another ambassador and example of fishing's upper crust. Kevin has fished professionally since 1990 and is one of the most decorated anglers in history. He won the BASS Angler of the Year Award on his very first year in the circuit and took the title again three more times. His hometown is Kalamazoo, Michigan, where he lives with his wife, Sherry, and their two kids. VanDam is known not only for being one of the most gifted anglers in the world and having the uncanny ability to catch fish in some of the toughest conditions, but also for being a great ambassador of the sport. His credits include winning the Bassmaster Classic in 2001 and 2005 and being voted the ESPN Sportsman of the Year in 2002. VanDam has 65 top 10 finishes on the Bass Tour and 12 tournament wins (as of August 2008 he had already won over $3 million), does seminars and is a product spokesperson for many companies in the United States. Tough to think that the ability to catch a lot of fish would make one famous, but VanDam has proven this to be true.

Chapter Three

Unique Fishing Destinations of North America

To properly cover the inside scoop on the fishing world, one must examine some of the more exotic and unique fishing destinations our countries have to offer. Just as the angler prepares himself to battle in the wilds of North America, so too must the water and land prepare to accept the angler. In this part of the world where water by sheer volume and surface area easily overshadows the land, there is a virtual cornucopia of lakes, streams, rivers and estuaries that boast healthy populations of freshwater and saltwater fish species. It's a fact that the destinations we have in our vast land to pursue the elusive fresh and saltwater fish are unique to this sport. From north to south, east to west, we are host to a staggering and unique selection of fishing lodges, outfitting operations, honey holes and other favorite haunts of the sportfishing community. This chapter will delve into some of the more noteworthy spots in some of the more off-the-beaten-path locations. As a great fisherman (my dad) once told me, "If a fishing hole is easy to get to, it's probably not worth fishing." It is a certain school of thought that the odd, unique or difficult-to-find areas are often the best. Sit back and let's travel across North America and see an array of the special and magnificent destinations—some of which I have visited personally—and others you or someone you know may have visited at one time or another.

Central Canada

Central Canada is not only the central hub of this great country in terms of population, but it accounts for some of the country's greatest and most noteworthy fishing waters, as well. This geographic region is home to a large chunk of the Great Lakes, including a portion of Lakes Superior, Huron, Ontario and Erie. It is also home to some of Canada's most impressive rivers. In Quebec, or La Belle Province as it has been called over the years, we see how this province has lived up to its lofty nickname. It is a place of an estimated one million lakes with fishing opportunities and destinations considered world renowned. It is also one of the most breath-takingly beautiful places in the country.

Fairmont Kenauk

With so much water and so many great lodges catering to the avid angler, the province of Quebec is one of North America's top destinations for sportfishing. For the trout enthusiast, there are such famous and historical lodges as the Fairmont Kenauk in Montebello. Kenauk, formally known as the Seigneurie Club and La Reserve de la Petite Nation, is not only the oldest hunting and fishing club in the province, but in all of North America as well. Kenauk dates back to the King of France who decreed that a parcel of land near the town of Montebello be set aside for enjoyment of outdoor recreation. Not only is Kenauk unique in its history and the clientele who were once members of this elite club, but the scenic splendor that still exists there today is a sight to behold. Kenauk's 65,000 acres or 100 square miles of protected wilderness, granted by King Louis XIV in 1674, is located halfway between the cities of Ottawa and Montreal and situated just north of the Ottawa River. Kenauk has more than 70 lakes on its territory, most of which are teeming with several species of trout: brook, rainbow, brown, lake and even the hybrid splake are found here. Not only has it welcomed guests into its territory since 1930 as a fully operational outfitting business, but Kenauk has also been the subject of many television shows and host to dozens of outdoor journalists over the years.

For folks like Kenauk's general manager, Bill Nowell, this wild haven has also become more than just a place of work. Nowell, on top of being a fish and wildlife biologist, is an accomplished fly fisherman. What better place to hone your skills as an angler than within the confines of one of North America's top private fishing domains?

Did you know?

The smallest fish in the world are the pygmy goby and the Luzon goby from the Philippines, which are only 1.5 inches long when they are full grown.

La Reserve Beauchene

Another important and unique fishing destination found in the province of Quebec is an outfitting operation called La Reserve Beauchene. Beauchene is, without a doubt, a true fisher's paradise. It is located in the Abitibi-Temiscaming region and spreads over 50,000 acres of prime Canadian wilderness. With more than 36 lakes on its territory, Beauchene has built a reputation for not only producing some of this country's top brook trout and smallmouth bass, but also for offering some of the most luxurious wilderness accommodations in North America. The area is unique in its angling opportunities for several reasons, one being its legendary brook trout fishing, something that has piqued the curiosity of many trout fanatics. Brook trout over five pounds are pulled from Beauchene waters with regularity and some specimens over seven pounds have even been caught. Thanks to sound fisheries management initiatives, this territory continues to produce quality fish today.

Another little-known fact of Beauchene lies in the strains of trout that swim in these Temiscaming waters. The famous Quebec red trout and Assinica strain are found in water bodies in and around the Beauchene territory. These peculiar strains of trout are unique in that they grow to enormous sizes and display beautiful colors during the fall spawn. These enormous trout are, in fact, a type of char that have adapted to the landlocked setting. Since most char are migratory and found in the tributaries of the North, these landlocked equivalents are quite special indeed. La Reserve Beuchene is another fine Quebec resort I discovered thanks to Gregory Cloutier of Quebec's Ministry of Tourism. In 2001, I co-hosted an episode of the *Officially Rugged with R.D.* fishing show at Beauchene the day of the World Trade Center tragedy. It was a bitter irony that after such an incredible trip with loads of great angling memories captured on film that at the same time the whole world was in mourning.

Here lies poor Thompson all alone, as dead and cold as any stone. In wading in the river Nith, he took a cold, which stopped his breath. He fish'd the stream for ten years past. Death caught him in his net at last.

Written on a tombstone in Dumphries, England.

–Tim Benn, *The Almost Compleat Angler*

Walsh on Ontario Fishing

Patrick Walsh, editor of Canada's biggest fishing and hunting magazine, *Outdoor Canada*, is one avid angler who is well aware of Ontario's prowess as a top fishing destination. He is also a man who's spent more than enough time on the water to know what he's talking about.

Walsh's favorite trout streams include the upper Ganaraska River for browns, brookies and rainbows; for big brown trout, he likes the Grand River; and for steelhead, the Maitland River is his first choice. When it comes to brook trout, splake and wild rainbows, the Haliburton lakes cannot be beat!

Patrick Walsh has his favorite haunts for other species as well, which he points out "aren't all necessarily the best hot spots in Ontario, although some are, but they're certainly places I enjoy fishing." For hauling in northern pike, Walsh usually heads to Lake Muskoka, Cook's Bay on Lake Simcoe or takes a short jaunt up to Georgian Bay. When it comes to smallmouth bass, he has a special affinity for Lake Simcoe, Lake Ontario and a couple of "secret" lakes in the Haliburton region he has kept under his hat.

For walleye, he enjoys the Bay of Quinte, and for largemouth bass Walsh likes Lake Scugog, located in Ontario's beautiful Kawartha Lakes Region. There are also some kettle lakes and farm ponds he has discovered on the Oak Ridges Moraine for largemouth. For the mighty muskellunge, he likes Lake of the Woods near Kenora as well as Lake Scugog, located a bit closer to his home. The province has some of the best variety fishing in all of North America and, as Walsh points out: "The cool thing about Ontario is that you never have to travel far to find decent fishing, and there's so much on offer."

Domaine Shannon Lodge

Another Quebec destination of note is the Domaine Shannon, located on the fringes of La Verendrye Park in Northwestern Quebec.

The Domaine Shannon is a family-run operation that covers 137 square miles of forest and waters nestled between the Cabonga and Baskatong Reservoirs. The Domaine Shannon, on top of being unique for its history and its appeal to hunters and anglers, is also special because of its northern pike and walleye fishing exploits. Shannon boasts more than 100 lakes within its territory, many of which are teeming with walleye and northern pike. The times that I have visited Domaine Shannon with my father in the past were memorable ones. We had no trouble hauling in sizable catches of the Quebec dore, or walleye, as they are known in the rest of North America, and northern pike of impressive sizes. Shannon is operated by the Danis family of Maniwaki, Quebec, who have dedicated their lives to the beautiful territory they run. Shannon territory is special to anyone who has ever visited it for its incredible angling opportunities and the chance to be pampered in a beautiful outdoor setting.

IT'S A FACT

In Tennessee it is illegal to catch fish by lasso.

Winter Fishing Destinations

The province of Ontario is home to some of the best winter fishing in all of North America. Once the cold weather arrives, thousands of crazy winter anglers suit up and head straight for the ice. One popular spot is eastern Ontario's fabled Bay of Quinte—one of this country's favorite locations for winter fishing. Quinte is what can only be described as a winter fishing mecca, as it has been producing world-class walleye for generations. Located two hours south of Ottawa in the Belleville-Nappanee area, Quinte still holds up to its legendary reputation. With the onslaught of zebra mussels in the Great Lakes over the years, the Bay has felt the effects with increased water clarity and changing walleye feeding patterns making it difficult to catch walleye during the day.

Most anglers have, however, learned to adapt and continue to reel in the big ones. Walleye over 10 pounds are nearly commonplace on the bay, and good numbers of fish can also be had on most outings. Ice conditions can sometimes be unstable, but once a solid footing is established, winter fishing enthusiasts cash in. Areas of greatest interest to most winter anglers are the Bay Bridge in Belleville, the Trenton area and Point Anne on the shore of Big Bay. Ice hut operators on the Bay of Quinte number in the dozens and generally offer the same services.

Ontario's Lake Simcoe is another ice fishing destination definitely worth its weight. Simcoe is host to over 5000 ice huts each winter with thousands of anglers in search of awesome cold water catches. Some of Lake Simcoe's largest fish are pulled out from the Jackson Point side, as Mike Wessell proved on March 28, 1999. Wessell, a Jackson's Point resident and experienced walleye angler, hauled in a behemoth 17-pound, 12-ounce specimen, which holds the "world record walleye taken through the ice with rod and reel" title. At the time, Wessell admitted that he has caught even larger walleye in Simcoe and just never bothered to have them registered, which goes to show that the next world record walleye may just be swimming in Simcoe waters. Something else to be aware of though is that Lake Simcoe is also famous for its pressure cracks,

a phenomenon caused when forming ice begins to shift during mid-winter creating huge, oftentimes impassable gaps.

Northwestern Ontario

Nowhere else in the world are the great outdoors and sportfishing as important to the community and to the heritage as in Northwestern Ontario. This vast region above Lake Superior, extending northward to the Manitoba border, is home to a myriad of water bodies. This region of Ontario is considered "God's country" to many and contains more Canadian Shield lakes than you can imagine. The fishing opportunities that exist in this area range from all members of the salmonidae, the esox or pike family, bass, walleye and every species in between. One unique aspect of Northwestern Ontario is the fact that fish and wildlife far outnumber the human population. Although there are various outfitting operations established on many of the lakes north of Lake Superior, as far northwest as Kenora and Lake of the Woods, people are few and far between. The shield waters of this region run cold, deep, steep-sided and are described by biologists as oligotrophic in nature. It is a part of the world they say, tongue-in-cheek, "the men are men and the moose are nervous."

*As the old fisherman remarked after explain-
ing the various ways to attach a frog to a hook,
it's all the same to the frog.*

–Paul Schullery, *Mountain Time*

Newfoundland & Labrador

Newfoundland & Labrador, located on Canada's far eastern fringe, is truly a different world unto itself. This ruggedly beautiful land is home to some of the country's most interesting characters as well as the ubiquitous moose, caribou, ptarmigan and—for those with a solid backbone—some of the best trout and Atlantic salmon fishing in entire the world. According to expert fisherman and editor of *Newfoundland Sportsman* magazine, Gord Follett, there are a few chosen locales one needs to visit when they're "in the neighborhood." Follett is a true "Newfie" born and bred and has been at the helm of the province's top hunting and fishing magazine for the past 18 years. He, along with its publisher, Dwight Blackwood, co-host a top-rated hunting and fishing television show by the same name—a series now entering its sixth season on the air.

According to Follet, to catch quality Atlantic salmon consistently, Eagle River is the place most islanders like to go. "You may not hook any 30-pounders," says Follett, "but the action is consistent during prime time, usually beginning in early-to-mid July."

Follet claims that for whatever reason, salmon on the Eagle are strong as hell and enjoy giving anglers a run for their money. "It could be proximity to the ocean or the cold water temperatures, but even the grilse (salmon under 25 inches) are powerful fighters and will take you into the backing," Follet explains. "Salmon in the 10- to 15-pound range are not uncommon; occasionally 20-plus pounders are hooked. And if you do hook a biggie between 15 and 20 pounds, you're in for the ride of your life," he adds.

Gord recounted the time during the summer of 2009 when *Newfoundland Sportsman* cameraman John Dyke lashed into a "medium-sized" fish between 15 and 18 pounds, and became physically and psychologically spent by the time he got the fish into the boat—some 45 minutes later.

For monster Atlantic salmon, Gord says Flower's River Lodge in Northern Labrador is the spot with fish up to 35 pounds, and 15- to 20-pounders are quite common. The lodge is located in an extremely remote part of Labrador and, during his six trips over the past 10 years, Gord claims he's never seen another living soul on the river outside of lodge guests.

Newfoundland's Humber River iseasily one of the world's most popular Atlantic salmon destinations, with fish in the 30- to 40-pound range hooked each year, says Follett. My own memories of the Humber River (which I will expand on in Chapter 4) can best be described as miraculous, and include an attempt to walk on water. But that's another story. At one particular spot on the river called Big Falls, located in a provincial park, Gord says visitors will sit on the rocks all day long to watch hundreds of leaping salmon make their way up the falls. It truly is a spectacular sight during the month of July.

For sheer fish numbers, Follett suggests the Exploits River in Central Newfoundland. The runs of returning salmon are consistently over 30,000 each year; this year, although it hasn't been officially confirmed just yet, it was closer to 35,000. For lake trout, he says, most people head to Labrador, where lakers in the 40- to 50-pound range are occasionally hooked. Gord once hooked a lake trout during the filming of the show that dragged his 12-foot boat and three men against the current before finally snapping his line. He has no idea how big the fish was, but will never forget the battle.

Another time while fishing at Newfoundland's Char Lake, a black bear decided he wanted Gord's fish for a snack, and wouldn't take no for an answer. Gord and TV co-host Dwight Blackwood kept shouting to scare the bruin off each time it came, but the bear got to within six feet and growled at them. Although still recuperating from knee surgery at the time, Gord says he could have beaten an Olympic champion long-jumper as he lunged backwards to get out of the way. Dwight, I am told, was so concerned for his pal's safety he could barely lift himself off the ground for several minutes from a fit of laughter. Those Newfies have a real crazy sense of humor!

Prince Rupert, British Columbia

Prince Rupert is a world-famous fishing destination and has some of the most productive salmon fishing waters in the world for giant king and coho salmon, as well as some of the largest Pacific halibut in existence. In Prince Rupert fishing is, without a doubt, a way of life. Residents of this beautiful region live close to the ocean and have not only immersed themselves in the beauty and splendor of this location but also in the angling opportunities it provides. The area has some very impressive statistics, including the home of the Pacific halibut that can grow to more than eight feet in length and weigh over 700 pounds. The Chinook, or spring salmon as they are referred to in Western Canada, can grow up to 60 pounds in Prince Rupert. A Chinook salmon weighing over 30 pounds is called a tyee. Prince Rupert also has a thriving coho salmon population, so anyone interested in pursuing these magnificent fish should do themselves a favor and head west. Ottawa-born Jeff Beckwith, a guide with the Blackfeather Fishing Charters, discovered this beautiful area of British Columbia 10 years ago, and has chosen to call it his home ever since. The operation Beckwith runs with his wife has been a successful one indeed, and he just loves to share his excitement of fishing in the area with his clients.

Every day I see the head of the largest trout
I ever hooked, but did not land.

–Theodore Gordon (1914)

The New England Coast

For anyone who has tried fishing off the New England Coast, it is an experience you will surely never forget. Fishing out of New Hampshire, Massachusetts and Maine provides anglers the opportunity to catch the highly sought-after striped bass or stripers, as they are commonly called. With the right tackle, it is also possible to catch stripers up and down the New England Coast—great sport for most anglers. These powerful fish will give anyone a run for their money and have helped give New England a reputation as a top sportfishing destination.

The bluefish is another important fish species and my personal favorite catch when visiting this region. Blues are a seasonal species and can be found in large feeding schools during late summer and early fall. Bluefish are incredibly aggressive feeders. I am told that even some New England beaches have closed due to foraging schools of bluefish in the area. If you are fortunate enough to get on a charter boat and connect with a feeding school of bluefish, it can only be described as "fishing mayhem." These powerful and aggressive feeders are known to shred fishing lines and tear bait apart like nobody's business. You haven't felt excitement until you've been on a boat with 30 people all battling bluefish at the same time.

Another calling card for the New England Coast is the tuna fishery. Bluefin, blackfin and yellowfin tuna are the heavyweights of the fishing world, with the bluefin reigning as king. The offshore charter boats who target bluefin out of such ports as Cape Anne in Gloucester, Massachusetts, and in around Cape Cod, Ipswitch Bay and the Isle of Shoals, are highly specialized fishing machines. The giant bluefin tuna are as powerful as they are elusive and have been dubbed by many as the ultimate saltwater fish. Once the tuna season kicks off each summer, anglers flock to the coast in search of yellowfin and possibly even bluefin tuna, using super heavy equipment including 100 pound-test fishing line, oversized Penn Senator fishing reels and hooks in the eight to ten size range.

Fishing for tuna is not only exciting, it can be extremely lucrative as well. Bluefin tuna, larger than 73 inches in length, may be sold at market and are highly prized by the Japanese. In most cases, the lucky angler will share in the profits along with the boat operator. Most bluefin that go to market sell for between $1000 and $10,000 while some giant bluefin have sold for over $100,000, and that's for just one fish! The bulk of the tuna is used to make sushi and various other dishes on the Asian market. The downside to the bluefin tuna fishing industry is, of course, the current state of the bluefin population. They are now considered a nearly threatened species, and fishing bans have been proposed over the past few years by conservationists in hopes of saving the remaining population of bluefin tuna lurking in these waters. According to analysts, it is all about money, since Japan puts out such a big amount to buy bluefin. Different interest groups around the world have been setting up meetings with the organization of Mediterranean countries calling for outright ban on bluefin fishing. It remains to be seen how this will affect the industry in New England but as with other popular fish, conservation is always of utmost importance.

The ancients wrote of the three ages of man; I propose to write of the three ages of the fisherman. When he wants to catch all the fish he can. When he strives to catch the largest fish. When he studies to catch the most difficult fish he can find, requiring the greatest skill and the most refined tackle, caring more for the sport than the fish.

–Edward R. Hewitt, *A Trout and Salmon Fisherman for Seventy-Five Years*

Adirondack Mountains

The Adirondack Mountains of upstate New York have been described as the Rocky Mountains of the U.S.A. east of the Mississippi River. Besides the scenic beauty creating a top destination for tourism in North America, the Adirondacks are known for clear lakes, cold mountain streams and some of the best trout and salmon fishing on the continent. There are a myriad of native trout and salmon rivers and lakes found within the Adirondack region, offering superb fishing opportunities to the fly-fishing enthusiast and spin caster alike. These range from the mountain lakes and streams in and around Lake Placid, Saranac Lake and Malone to the north, down to the larger bodies of water such as Lake George in the more southern areas of the park. Although known as a salmon hotspot, the Adirondacks are better known for trout fishing opportunities. Anglers come from all around to fish the famous Ausable River for brown and rainbow trout, as well as the for spring and fall runs of landlocked salmon.

Florida Keys

Mention the Florida Keys, and one instantly pictures a gentle, warm ocean breeze, Jimmy Buffet music and some of the most celebrated saltwater fishing anywhere in the world. The Keys are located between the Gulf of Mexico, the Atlantic Ocean and the Florida Bay. The Gulf Stream, with its warm currents running in and around Florida Bay and the Keys, makes for a perfect migration spot for many fish species. Most fishing guides in the area will concentrate in and around Key West, as far away as Key Largo and anywhere up and down the 120-mile stretch of the Florida Keys.

The peculiar humps located along the continental shelf, called seamounts, are like rising sunken islands. These seamounts are remnants of ancient volcanoes and provide excellent habitat for the area's fish population. Many charter boats target these areas around the keys to catch grouper, amberjack, dolphin fish, Oahu, marlin, barracuda, bonita and a variety of other popular Florida game fish. The great thing about the Florida Keys, besides the favorable weather and scenic splendor of this

ocean paradise, is the ability to sneak in and around protected flats on a rough day. Since the ocean can become quite rough, reef fishing and casting around sunken shipwrecks is another favorite for those who enjoy using light tackle, giving the Florida Keys the title of the "Gulf's Fishing Paradise" and another unique fact and feature of fishing in North America.

Yet fish there be, that neither hook nor line nor snare, nor net, nor engine can make thine.

–John Bunyan, *Pilgrim's Progress*

Columbia River

Sturgeon fishing on western North America's mighty Columbia River has become the stuff of legends. The sturgeon is our largest and most famous freshwater game fish, with the ability to reach lengths of 15 feet and more. In the Columbia River of the Western United States and Canada, it is the white sturgeon that draws trophy anglers from around the world. The white sturgeon is a dinosaur in both age and gargantuan size. The mystery and allure that surround the sturgeon is what attracts eager people from far and wide. It is a unique-looking fish with no teeth and four barbels on the underside of its snout. There are rows of diamond shaped scales on its body, which are known as scutes. These scutes can be very sharp and act as a deterrent against predators.

As far as the Columbia River goes, resident sturgeon come in three different size classes: the shakers, the keepers and the peelers. A shaker is a sturgeon under 42 inches in length and must always be released unharmed. The shaker gets its name from what it does when it is hooked to an angler's rod. They will create a shake and vibration indicating the smaller size. The keeper fish is any sturgeon in the Columbia measuring between 42 to 60 inches; the keeper-size fish is a size seen regularly on the Columbia. This size can be kept for consumption although it is not recommended that any sturgeon be kept as their stocks are extremely fragile.

Finally, the third type is the peeler. As its name implies, it can peel all the line off the angler's reel in no time. Conventional tackle will not hold these fish, and they are seldom seen by the average angler. The white sturgeon fishery of the Columbia relies heavily on the shad fish as forage—the larger the shad the larger the peeler sturgeon. To properly fish these oversized Goliaths, extremely heavy and large tackle is required as well as a boat with quick-release anchors and a crew in the habit of catching peeler-size sturgeon. The Columbia River is unique in the history of peeler sturgeon that it has seen. The Internet is regularly host to giant sturgeon photos, more than 10, 11, 12 or even 14 feet in length and pushing 1000 pounds. It is illegal to keep any fish of this size, and those in the sturgeon industry would frown upon ever harming one of these majestic dinosaurs.

My elation at taking that particular fish was quite beyond rational justification. I experienced an illusion of triumph which contained not only the impression that I had finally succeeded in outfoxing a shrewd and calculating adversary, but that the trout had been made to know the humiliation of defeat.

–Harold Blaisdell, *The Philosophical Fisherman*

Alaska: The Final Frontier

The state of Alaska, with its northern latitude and arctic-like conditions, is very different than the rest of continental United States. Life north of the 60th parallel is unique indeed. While mining, tourism and logging make up a large part of the region's top industries, hunting and fishing account for the bulk of Alaska's economy. The state is known for its world-class salmon fishing. Like Prince Rupert, it has some of the best Chinook fishing in the world. It is a place where the rivers run cold and thick with spawning Pacific salmon and terrain so rugged that only experienced sportsmen would dare go. Sitka is perhaps the most popular salmon area in all of Alaska. Migrating fish tend to linger in Sitka, offering fly fishermen and women a good chance at hooking one of these magnificent fish. Sitka is known for having a higher angling success rate than other areas of the state and is therefore a fishing hotspot.

For sheer size, the Kenai River has some of the largest king salmon around, weighing upward of 100 pounds! Kodiak Island is another top fishing destination, because as they say on the island, 3500 brown bears can't be wrong. The oversized bruins which "bear" the island's name have become so huge simply because they dwell in an area with copious numbers of spawning salmon to feed on. Kodiak is also said to provide the best roadside salmon fishing in the entire state, with many rivers easily accessible by car. On top of the world-class salmon fishing opportunities in Alaska, there is fantastic lake trout, brook trout and Dolly Varden fishing there as well. I am told that one trip into Alaska is like a voyage into

a lifestyle that existed a century ago. Since fishing has always been such an important resource activity in Alaska, there are hundreds of fishing lodges and guides available to anyone with the urge for a once in a lifetime adventure.

Kaminsky's Top Ten Fishing Destinations

According to Peter Kaminsky of TopTen.com, there are several spots around the world worthy of the title of best fishing destination, and the bulk of these lie in North America. Number eight on Kaminsky's list is the Ozark Mountains of Missouri in the United States. Kaminsky recalls the beauty and splendor of catching smallmouth bass under the limestone bluffs on the Winding River of the Ozarks. Apparently it doesn't matter which river you choose, as all of these streams offer excellent angling, and as Kaminsky points out, "The Sandy Spits are witness to huge fish migrations."

Number six on Kaminsky's list is Yellowstone National Park in Wyoming, and as indicated on his list, although the Park does receive millions of visitors each year, the quality of the trout fishing there is still second to none. Yellowstone includes several stocked streams with good populations of trout, while the native streams like Slough Creek provide trophy-sized trout angling and the nearby streams in Montana, Idaho and Wyoming are also legendary.

Number four is Newfoundland & Labrador, and although we have covered this region, it is interesting to see how it rates on a worldwide scale. Kaminsky notes how brook trout reign supreme in these northern waters and how they can grow to enormous sizes in this short Canadian summer. He also points out that Newfoundland & Labrador is a center for fly-fishing. When the wind is down and the sun is out, the brookies will strike flies, usually the larger ones.

Number two on his list is Manitoba, and he notes that although the Canadian northern pike are fast and furious predators and can be easily caught below the 49th parallel, they seem to grow meaner and larger in the province of Manitoba, where the giant northerns can tear a strip off a fly rod in no time.

This brings us to number one on the all time best fishing destinations list according to TopTen. com, and that location is Montauk Point in New York State. It is noted that many naturalists feel that more fish swim by the tip of Long Island than any other spot on earth. Species including marlin, tuna, striped bass, cod, mackerel and the great white shark all pass within a lure's cast of New York State's oldest and most famous lighthouse. Kaminsky also notes that on the rocks below the lighthouse beacon, anglers can experience possibly the world's top surfcasting.

American Fly-fishing Hot Spots

Since fly-fishing is such an avid sport, and historical as well, the popular fly-fishing hot spots in the United States should be mentioned here. The Colorado River has been identified as perhaps the best destination for rainbow trout. These spunky, colorful fish can be caught almost year round in the various reaches of the Colorado River and especially in the stretch of water that runs between Glen Canyon Dam and the upper end of the Grand Canyon. Even though trout are the calling card here in Colorado, some fly fishers may opt for the oversized carp that lurk in the flat areas.

Another hotspot in the U.S. is Gunpowder Falls in the state of Maryland. This is a hotspot for coldwater trout in the Southeast, as trout stocking programs have flourished here over the years. Maryland state and Trout Unlimited teamed up to release various strains of wild trout to mix with the native stock, which has produced fabulous brown, brook and rainbow trout opportunities. The Gunpowder Falls State Park is one area of note.

The Driftless area in Wisconsin is another fabulous fly-fishing area with some superb brown trout streams. The counties in the southwest of Wisconsin produce fabulous catches of trout in streams galore. Lake CW McConaughy in Nebraska is the largest lake in that state and is home to some of the best fly-fishing available anywhere. Freemont Lakes State Park in Nebraska also provides some excellent fly-fishing opportunities. Pennsylvania is also known for its great trout fishing opportunities and most of the streams remain cool, even in the summertime. Fishing Creek, as it is called, appears to be a popular fly-fishing area in the specific five-mile stretch called the Narrows, where wild trout are pulled out on a regular basis. Laguna Madre in Texas is another area loaded with excellent fly-fishing opportunities in addition to the Southern Texas Coast, which has some great saltwater opportunities and some flats near Padre Island that house a plethora of fish species just lying in wait.

For the avid fly angler, the United States also has dozens of other fabulous destinations not mentioned here, many of which have been kept under somebody's hat as some of the old-school anglers tend to keep their secret spots to themselves.

Chapter Four

Incidents and Accidents: Fishing Horror Stories

With all of its benefits and many positive attributes, fishing as a recreational activity still carries with it a downside. It is, in fact, one of the most dangerous activities on earth, and the statistics are there to prove it. Although the inherent goodness and benefits of this sport still ring true, it can be a perilous journey. Factors such as deep water, boating troubles, cold weather and hypothermia, accidents with fishing tackle and strong water current all play a part in making this activity not only weird and wonderful but downright dangerous! Regardless of whether you're doing some offshore angling for bluefish or casting for steelhead in the gin clear waters of Alberta, incidents and accidents are more commonplace than many people realize.

Bill Barilko

Perhaps the most famous and horrific fishing-related tale of them all is the story of Bill Barilko.

William "Bashin' Bill" Barilko was a hockey player born in Timmins, Ontario, in 1927. He spent much of his pro career with the Toronto Maple Leafs and was, in fact, one of the Leafs' top players at the time. In the span of five seasons, the Leafs won four Stanley Cups, making Bill Barilko a household name in the late 1940s. Besides having a promising hockey career, Barilko was also an avid fisherman, and in the summer of 1951, he and his friend Henry Hudson flew to Sioux River, Quebec, in Hudson's Fairchild 24. On the way home, after enjoying several days of fresh northern Quebec air, their single engine plane disappeared completely, and Barilko and Hudson went missing. It was not until 11 years later, on June 7, 1962, that the wreckage of Barilko's plane was discovered in Northern Ontario. The crash was believed to be caused by poor weather, overloaded cargo and possibly pilot inexperience. Ironically, during the course of the 11 years that Barilko was missing, the Toronto Maple Leafs never won another Stanley Cup until 1962 when Barilko's body was finally discovered. The Canadian rock band The Tragically Hip paid tribute to the sad fishing trip in their song "Fifty-Mission Cap," which tells the tale of Bill Barilko. The Barilko story is just one of many dark and mysterious clouds that hang over fishing today, and it remains one of the most mysterious events in Canadian history.

The Red Cross Study

According to a 10-year study carried out by the Red Cross in May 2009, fishing ranked as the top cause of drowning-related deaths in Canada between 1991 and 2000. The study highlighted the popularity of sportfishing as a Canadian pastime and that it has led to a high percentage of drowning deaths. Over the 10-year period, 84 percent of all victims were boating at the time of their death; nine percent were on shore; four percent were ice fishing; and three percent were standing out in the water fishing. It seems that fishing-related deaths while out on the water also show a regional disparity, with the majority of victims being in British Columbia and the Atlantic provinces. Often, those who drowned were not wearing floatation devices and, of course, the bitterly cold Canadian water and hypothermia were also contributing causes. According to the Canadian Red Cross, six factors must be considered when venturing outdoors for a day of fishing: cold weather, bad weather, poor swimming ability, alcohol intake, water current and lack of flotation. If these six factors are considered, and measures are taken, fewer deaths would occur. An avid angler myself, I know full well the dangers of fishing and water-related accidents. While salmon fishing on the Humber River in 1981, I was nearly swept down by the current when my chest waders filled with water. The weight pulled me to the river bottom like a stone, but fortunately my father was there to rescue me and pull me to safety. This is just one example of how quickly accidents can happen while enjoying your favorite activity.

Did you know?

Minnows have teeth located on a bone in their throat.

Keep your Eye on the Lure

It is common knowledge that casting a sharp lure and other fishing plugs rigged with hooks can be a dangerous activity. One must take extra precaution when casting and fishing in close proximity to other anglers. In the United States, fishing recently outranked basketball as the leading cause of eye injury and admittance to emergency rooms across the country. It's hard to imagine the effects of getting a lure hooked in the eye by a friend or with your own fishing line. The size and sharpness of the hooks available on most fishing tackle today make it especially dangerous when you are struck in the face with one. A typical fishhook is designed in such a way that a barb acts like a doorstop when the point is struck into the fish's mouth during hook set. This barb also creates catastrophic damage when a hook is accidentally impaled into someone's skin, or even worse, an eyeball. Oftentimes, a doctor will have no choice but to surgically cut away the hook, leaving the person permanently blind. Certain measures can be taken to prevent eye injury while fishing. Each angler must always allow a fishing arm's length around him or her while casting. Regardless of whether you're casting from a boat, from shore or from a fishing dock, allowing yourself more room to maneuver will always prevent accidents, especially those freak accidents that you never see coming. Protective eyewear, of course, will also prevent eye injury in the event of a lure gone astray. Many anglers today outfit themselves with the latest polarized glasses, allowing them to see better on the water and also helping to prevent serious injury. Another important thing to remember is always to keep your eye on the lure. Good casting control will make for a safer fishing day for you and others around you. Although it may be a bit of a cliché, Mom always claimed it was "all fun and games until someone loses an eye!"

Don't Give Me No Lip!

As a father of two budding anglers, there are many lessons I have learned over the years through trial and error. Unfortunately, some lessons came the hard way. As I strive to raise my two girls to follow in my path of making the most of our outdoor recreational activities, I often encounter the odd pitfall along the way.

Back in 2004, while preparing for a day of fishing with my daughters, I learned a valuable lesson about fishing rods and hook control. As I gathered earthworms and rigged our fishing rods for a morning of sunfish on a nearby lake, I made the false assumption that my four-year-old was responsible enough to handle a fishing rod with a hook on it. Just as we were about to leave for Lake McDonald, my old friend showed up to say "Hi," and I took my eyes off my daughter, Grace, for a moment. While she sat in the back seat of the vehicle waiting to go, fishing rod held between her legs, I chatted briefly with my pal. Without thinking, Grace decided to chew on the end of her fishing rod, not realizing that I had reeled the hook and sinker to the end of the rod thinking they would be tucked away safe and sound.

Seconds later, we heard screams coming from the back seat as my older daughter, Emily, yelled to me that Grace had been hooked like a fish. "Hooked like a fish?" I asked. As I rushed to the car, the horror of my four-year-old attached to the end of her fishing rod with a hook protruding out of her lip was too much to bear. Although it was small, the number six snelled hook is extremely sharp, and she had driven the barb deep into the flesh of her lower lip. Fortunately, I had experience with being jabbed myself on occasion, so I retrieved a pair of pliers and was able to push the barb through and cut off the end. Even though the ordeal was a freak accident and lasted less than five minutes, barely leaving a mark on the inside of her lip, it was a lesson well learned on the perils of fishing tackle. My daughter and I are both more careful now when it comes to fishing rods and sharp hooks.

An elderly member of a distinguished fishing club...became so bored during the winter closed season that he used to take his fly boxes to bed. The wife plucking an errant Blue Charm from a sensitive part of her anatomy, possibly in the dead of night, had a legitimate complaint. His wife, a good woman at heart, allowed him back into her bed, with his boxes, providing he counted his flies before and after.

–Conrad Voss Bark, *A Fly on the Water*

The Deadliest Job
Commercial fishermen and women have the dubious distinction of being some of the hardest

working and most accident prone of any anglers in the world. The Alaskan crab fishery, as lucrative and exciting as it is, has also been called the most dangerous job in the world today. These commercial crabbers are a different breed, having to deal with sub-zero temperatures in the Bering Strait, working out of Dutch Harbor—the largest port in the United States—in the most God-awful conditions. There are many causes and reasons for danger and fluke accidents in this industry. If you can imagine a 130-foot vessel with a 75-foot crab pot boom swinging around like a pendulum at eye level throughout most of the season, you can see how people get hurt! Injury can occur anywhere in a crab fisher's day. If the sub-zero temperatures of the Bering Strait don't get you, there are a number of other hazards where death and injury lurk around every corner. Deck hands who handle the crab pots are prone to getting caught up in ropes and lines and must deal with the motion of 30-foot seas. Crab fishing crew have been thrown overboard and have had fingers and hands torn off in freak accidents of which there are too many to measure.

Commercial crab fishing has been dubbed "the worst job with the best pay" and if you have ever watched the television series *The Deadliest Catch*, you will quickly understand where that expression comes from. In 2006 alone, some 500 commercial fishers in Alaska hauled in $126 million worth of crab. Although that averages $250,000 per person, keep in mind that the captain and boat owner account for more than half of that income. The salary for the industry's 36,000 employees is

reported at the bureau of labor statistics in the U.S. as averaging just $27,250 per year. Keep in mind that there are disparities among the fishers as far as catch goes. As with any fishing, the old expression that 10 percent of the anglers account for 90 percent of the fish is not too far off when it comes to crab fishing. Why do they do it then? From what I have witnessed, it is more than just the intrigue of a fat paycheck. The excitement and challenge of tackling Mother Nature in some of the world's harshest conditions is, perhaps, the personal challenge of lifetime. It tests intestinal fortitude and takes certain strength of character and commitment to be successful as a commercial angler, and as wacky as it sounds, it seems there is nothing these brave people would rather do. The same can be said about anglers everywhere, if you ask me.

Winter Fishing Perils

In the Northern Hemisphere, winter fishing in an activity enjoyed by many and continues to be a fun and challenging sport in the colder months. Ice fishing is synonymous with Canada and the Northern United States as few other activities are available for the avid sportsman at this time of year. Let's face it, though, ice fishing is a strange and dangerous sport. The techniques and strategies required to ice fish are completely unique and different than required at other times of the year, and ice angers themselves are a strange bunch indeed. These are the folks who have no difficulty spending long hours on a frozen lake or river holding a small fishing rod and waiting for some action to start. I know many diehard winter anglers who think nothing of heading out on the ice in −5, −20 and even −40°F. These are fanatics who use special ice fishing vehicles to get to their favorite spot—vehicles with the doors completely removed. In case they ever fall through the ice, a safer escape is available to them. These are the people who think nothing of spending the night in an ice hut measuring a mere four feet by eight feet, feeling more like a prison cell than a cabin.

Ice anglers have a strange and eerie connection to their sport and an abnormal dedication. I believe the sense of danger involved in ice fishing is part of its appeal. There are so many pitfalls to the sport of winter angling such as ice conditions, the risk of hypothermia and even the risk of carbon monoxide poisoning from improperly ventilated heating equipment in fishing huts. So why do they do it? I suppose the challenge in catching fish during the wintertime and battling Mother Nature to be successful are the motivating factors. Ice anglers are infamous for stranding themselves on the ice as a result of pressure cracks and unsafe ice conditions. Here are a few tales of bravery and blatant disregard for safety—all in the name of winter fishing.

Stranded Like Harp Seals

The largest and most famous ice fishing rescue story occurred in February 2009 when 150 ice fishers from Ohio made the ill-advised decision one morning to use a small plank of wood as a makeshift bridge to cross an open pressure crack on Lake Erie. The anglers crossed the pressure crack, which exposed six to eight feet of open water, using boards that allowed them to reach the fishing area farther out on the lake. The problem was that the high winds and unstable ice caused the outer section of the lake to separate from the shore, and the once six-foot gap soon became several hundred yards of open water, leaving all 150 of them stranded like harp seals on an ice floe. Since winter anglers don't tend to get worked up over much, things were fine until the end of the day when they all wanted to return to the shore and realized that they were stranded. The largest ever helicopter recovery mission of people stranded on ice was put into effect, leaving both the American and Canadian officials scratching their heads. One man even died as a result. So then, why did they do it? These folks were so determined to fish that common sense was pushed aside and a convoluted logic took over in building a bridge across ice cold open water to gain access to a better fishing spot. As summed up perfectly by the Toledo Police Department, "If there was a section in the code about common sense, we'd have 150 arrest warrants out there today."

…there is nothing clinical about fishing…there is nothing about it that can be viewed in a clinical vacuum. Everything—as in everything else— relates to everything else; and the deeper down one goes, the nearer the quick of life one draws.

–Brian Clarke, *The Pursuit of the Stillwater Trout*

Trip Ends Poorly

I believe every angler has a personal tale of a weird and scary near-death experience. For me, it was May 29, 1993. After enjoying a week of excellent trout fishing in Quebec's Zec Lesueur, north of St. Anne du Lac, my trip ended in near tragedy. As I sat by the bonfire with my father, Rathwell, and brothers-in-law, Bruce and Steve, an eerie sense of calm came over us as we discussed our plans for the next year's trip. Hashing and rehashing our annual fishing trips was something we did on the final night; however, this year we did so without realizing that the next day we would have a brush with death. As we packed up the truck the next morning, Bruce and I were reminded of a moment of indiscretion during the trip when we put a large gouge on the back of my father's new Toyota pickup. "Man, we are never going to live that down," I said to Bruce, as we picked up the last few scraps around our tent area. Perhaps that foreshadowed what was about to happen. Traveling south on the highway past a town called Lac St. Paul, all of a sudden, out of the corner of our eyes, a large tractor-trailer hauling a D-8 bulldozer appeared out of nowhere, heading right out across the highway in front of us.

The moment was surreal; my father only had time to swerve, but being so weighted down with a loaded truck, a trailer, a four wheeler and two canoes, stopping quickly was impossible. The semi struck our vehicle midway down the passenger side and crumpled it like a tin can. Bruce fortunately had enough sense to dive in the opposite direction as the bulk of the contact was felt in his corner. The tractor-trailer tore out the entire side of our truck and sent all of us to the hospital.

How quickly a wonderful fishing adventure can go from joyous to disaster. Fortunately for us, it was not our time as we all suffered only minor injuries. This may be my weird and unexpected brush with death, but there are many other fishing-related incidents just like mine out there. These accidents are, unfortunately, part and parcel of the sport itself. Fishing requires a lot of traveling and our roads and highways are a dangerous place. Although it has been 16 years since the accident, we barely speak of it today and have never returned to the area to fish. I always felt the accident was a sign for us to find another area to fish.

…you will search far to find a fisherman to admit that a taste for fishing, like a taste for liquor, must be governed lest it come to possess its possessor…

–Sparse Grey Hackle, *"Murder" Fishless Days*

Toothy Fishing Hazards

Bear attacks are one fishing hazard often overlooked by many avid anglers and wrongly so. Since many of the backwoods fishing spots in

North America are found in the heart of bear country—be they black bear or grizzly—and extra vigilance should be used at all times. With these bruins emerging from hibernation and on the prowl for food, bear encounters are more frequent during spring and pose an undeniable risk to anglers.

One very sad example of bear vs. fisherman is the Quebecker who was fatally attacked by a bear in May 2008, during a spring fishing excursion. Cecile Lavoie and her husband were fishing their favorite walleye hole near La Sarre, Quebec, when, after being separated from her husband, the 73-year-old grandmother was dragged into the forest by a rogue black bear. Mr. Lavoie chased the bear for some distance and managed to scare the animal away from his wife. He was unable to carry her bleeding body back to safety, so he decided to run for help. When he returned to the area later with police, the same bear confronted them aggressively. For unknown reasons, Quebec police chose to wait until morning to continue the search, and they discovered Cecile Lavoie's lifeless body. Her devastated husband said his wife of 51 years was an angel who lived to hunt and fish.

It is an unfortunate and rare fishing situation that does occur every year. We can, however, do things to protect ourselves. While walking in bear country, make sure to announce your presence by breaking brush, walking loudly and traveling in groups. Aerosol deterrents like bear spray should be carried at all times while traveling to and from your favorite trout lake or river. During portages on the trail, always assign the first person in the group as bear spray operator. They must have their hands free and their eyes open. Black bear encounters are rare but dangerous hazards of early season fishing, and we should be prepared.

Drowning Danger Well Documented

An extensive study carried out in Australia in 2008 looked at fishing from a safety standpoint, where researchers sighted various risk factors involved in one of the country's favorite pastimes. Marine research consultant, Julian Pepperell, produced a paper called "Recreational Fishing and Safety in Australia." The paper looks at risk factors and injuries related to fishing and seeks ways to improve the safety of this favorite sport. According to Pepperell, the majority of fishing-related deaths in Australia have to do with drowning, and data compiled from this study revealed that a staggering 140 fishing-related accidental drownings occurred between 2000 and 2007. The study went on to show that many injuries related to recreational fishing are never actually documented and that many near-death experiences, and those that do not actually result in hospital stays, are often never recorded. Of the hospital data that was gathered to complete this study, reports indicate that cuts, usually from fish hooks, fish bites and falling are the major causes of injuries and account for 72 to 89 percent of all the fishing injuries in Australia. The researcher continues to sift through statistics with hopes of disseminating information whereby anglers may increase the safety of the sport in Australia.

Commercial Fishing Accidents in Canada

The Transportation Safety Board of Canada is the agency responsible for monitoring marine safety, which includes commercial fishing, and in their most recent report of entitled "Statistical Summary—Marine Occurrences," the number of deaths that directly result from marine accidents and commercial fishing are documented and compared with the previous 10 years' statistics. In 2006, 467 marine accidents were documented, which is actually 22 fewer than the previous year. Marine accidents actually reached a 30-year low in 2006, as the 10-year average was 506 per year. The marine-related fatalities in 2006 totaled 18, two less than the previous year and seven less than the 10-year average of 25. Of these fatalities, the bulk of deaths were the result of fishing vessel accidents.

The most frequent type of marine accidents is groundings, accounting for 26 percent of all accidents, and also include flooding, striking and peril directly related to the vessel itself. In 2006, Canada had a total of 20,000 fishing vessels, which represents 74 percent of all registered boats excluding pleasure craft. Since 1997, approximately 50 percent of all vessels involved in accidents have been fishing vessels. In 2006, 208 fishing vessels were involved in accidents, compared to 237 the year before. So there is no doubt that commercial fishing is a dangerous profession, although the silver lining on this cloud seems to indicate that safety is on the increase.

"Crocodile Hunter" Steve Irwin

The death of world famous filmmaker and television host "Crocodile Hunter" Steve Irwin on September 4, 2006, was perhaps the most famous marine- and fish-related fatality of all. Irwin was pierced in the chest by a stingray spine while snorkeling in Australia off the Great Barrier Reef. He lost consciousness and died a short time later. The events were caught on camera, and the footage was actually handed to Australian authorities who surmised that the stingray felt threatened by Irwin and his cameraman being so close. The animal flexed its tail and drove the 10-inch long serrated spine into Irwin's heart. Instinctively, Irwin pulled the spine out before losing consciousness. The accident was deemed to be a nearly one-in-a-million fluke; however, a similar accident occurred in Florida a month later. In that case, the man survived a stingray barb through the heart, suggesting that Irwin's removal of the barb might have actually hastened his death.

...there is great pleasure in being on the sea, in the unknown wild suddenness of a great fish; in his life and death which he lives for you in an hour while your strength is harnessed to his; and there is satisfaction in conquering this thing which rules the sea it lives in.

–Ernest Hemingway, *On the Blue Water*

Geographical Distribution of Commercial Fishing Accidents

According to statistics in 2006 for Canada, 72 percent of all marine accidents occurred in three specific geographical regions: the Western region accounted for 30 percent, the Maritime region for 24 percent and Newfoundland & Labrador region for 18 percent. As a whole, these regions are responsible for the bulk of commercial fishing accidents. As commercial fishing accidents dominate the coastal waters, it is encouraging at least to see that they are on the decline. It is my belief that, as technology increases and techniques become more refined, the safety of our commercial fishing industry will also improve.

Take One for the Noble Beast

During a typical overcast July morning, Sean Landsman and Matt Clay were headed to their favorite muskie spot in search of a specimen for Landsman's project "Noble Beast." Biologist Sean Landsman is working on the research project in partnership with Muskies Canada Inc. (MCI) and Muskies Inc. of the United States, as well as other special interest groups. The project is an ongoing study looking at the post-released mortality rates and movement of the mighty muskellunge. Matt Clay, being an avid muskie angler, was quick to volunteer his skills to the cause. After all, it was for the betterment of a fish species Matt has been pursuing for decades. As the two began to set up shop in their favorite muskie haunt, Sean joked that he only had a few radio tags, and therefore they would probably be in for a blockbuster day. Within minutes, Sean's line jerked, and a fish was on and headed towards the net. After he took some measurements and blood samples, he attached a tag and released Mr. Muskie safely back into the river. Since it was early in the morning and only two radio transmitters were left, they had hoped they would put one on a mid-30-pound fish. "Let's make the next one count!" Sean said as they aimed their casts towards a large weed flat. Two or three short casts later and Matt had a heavy strike.

"Fish on, but this time it's a biggie!" he said, and a 50-inch plus healthy female fish made its way to the net. The boys always used only the best equipment and proper handling techniques as part of this study; however, this girl was strong and one tremendous headshake during the hook-out process, and the thud sound and feeling meant only one thing. Matt was attached to an angry 30-pound muskie, which was connected to a number five treble hook, and neither Matt nor the muskie was too happy about it.

"It's past the barb," he yelled out to Sean. Fortunately, the next headshake from the old girl dislodged the hook from the fish's mouth. Unfortunately though, the hook was still lodged in Matt's hand. As they grabbed the Nipex hook-cutting tools, a quick snap and Matt's hand was free of the gigantic muskie lure, as free as one can be with a large part of the hook still embedded in your finger. The boys had to make a decision as to whether to process the fish or not. Since the importance of the study outweighed the pain that Matt felt, they decided to radio track her as usual and proceeded to follow her for the next four hours, monitoring her post catch movement. Once the study was complete on the final fish of that day, the boys made a trip to the emergency room, and it was easy to tell that this hook was not going to be easy to remove. After copious amounts of painkillers and two needles, the two doctors were able to dislodge the nasty piece of steel from Matt's hand. Thanks to proper techniques and equipment, Matt Clay has no long-term effects from his hooking. They thank their lucky stars that they had the proper bolt-cutting tool with them as both Matt and the fish managed to make it with out any long-term damage. I'd say, though, the fish made out better than Matt did!

IT'S A FACT

Fishing from the back of an animal is illegal in Idaho.

Personal Injury Lawyers

With over 300 million residents in the United States of America and a large proportion of recreational sportfishing enthusiasts, it is little wonder that fishing accidents abound in this country. In California, for example, sportfishing and charter boat accidents are so common that personal injury lawyers are now specializing in them. The law firm of Banning, Micklow and Bull in Oakland, California, specialize in maritime trial law, sportfishing and charter boat claims. According to B, M & B, injuries of this nature neither fall under the Jones Act—a law covering commercial fishers—nor are they covered under the cruise ship passengers' related laws. In their experience, plaintiffs must seek to establish some type of negligence on the part of the charter boat operator, and injuries they've seen vary greatly from drowning and injuries while on deck to lacerations and cuts from onboard equipment. In the case of negligence on board, this law firm seeks to establish a prior knowledge of a dangerous condition as well as establish liability on the part of the boat operator. If you are a commercial angler, Banning, Micklow and Bull may also be able to help you as they understand the California marine laws and can represent anyone who has been injured in this sport.

I suppose it comes down to the old law of supply and demand. If there were no injuries, there would be no need for a law firm to represent the injured, and vice versa. In this case, it appears the supply of fishing-related injuries and associated lawsuits are enough to warrant the need of a lawyer. Personal injury lawyers who specialize in fishing-related accidents are just another weird and wonderful fact of the world of fishing.

It's time to dust off the tackle, pull out the waders and head for the stream. But not so fast. Spring in Canada can be a tumultuous time in the outdoors, with winter slowly giving way to longer days and warmer weather. For trout enthusiasts, that often means dealing with copious hazards, from lingering ice to cranky bears emerging from their dens.

–Jeff Morrison, "Early Season Trout Troubleshooting Guide," *Outdoor Canada Magazine*

Safety Stats in the United States

The 2006 statistics report on fishing and recreational boating indicated that alcohol use is the number one contributing factor to fatal boating and fishing accidents, accounting for 20 percent of all reported fatalities. There is little doubt that, as with driving a vehicle, alcohol and boating, and therefore fishing, does not make a good mix. In the United States, the Coast Guard Auxiliary along with their partners offer informative courses, similar to the boaters course in Canada, on safe boating, proper etiquette and rules while fishing on the water. In 2006 alone, 710 people died in boating- and fishing-related incidents, and it was determined that those anglers who did not take the U.S. Coast Guard Auxiliary course stood a substantially greater chance of dying on the water. It was also noted that in the United States since the year 2000, the average fatality rate of anglers and boaters has ranged between 5.3 and 5.8 deaths per 100,000 registered boats. During the previous decade, that rate ran as high as 8.3 deaths per 100,000 boaters. The slight increase in the safety factor has been observed across North America and can be attributed to safety courses like this one offered in the U.S. and in Canada.

We who go a-fishing are a peculiar people. Like other men and women in many respects, we are like one another, and like no others, in other respects. We understand each other's thoughts by and intuition of which we know nothing. We cast our flies on many waters, where memories and fancies and facts rise, and we take them and show them to each other, and small or large, we are content with our catch.

–W.C. Prime, *I Go A-Fishing*

Ice-fishing Muskrat Hole

Of all the years that Deb Brown of Osgoode, Ontario, has been out fishing and hunting, she always had a sense that someone was watching out for her. Deb has been one of the fortunate few outdoor enthusiasts to have enjoyed the great outdoors over the years without very many mishaps. There have been a few close calls though, like the time she was ice fishing in the Ottawa Valley. Brown was at a cottage for the weekend, and first thing Saturday morning, Deb and her two friends headed out onto the frozen lake with an ice auger and a bucket full of tip ups. There was a fresh blanket of snow covering the ice from the night before, so no tracks or previous fishing activity were visible on the lake. Deb's partner was in the lead, carrying the gas auger, and the other two anglers followed behind him. All of a sudden, without warning, Deb saw the ice auger fly from his arms as he plunged through the ice. Deb's friend was, fortunately, wearing an old Woods parka, which helped insulate him and acted like a flotation device enabling him to crawl out and roll across the ice looking a bit like the Michelin Man.

It had all happened so fast that none of them realized their friend had actually fallen through a hole that had been nicely maintained by a family of muskrats. Luckily, Deb's pal had the reflexes and the where-with-all to roll with it instead of going straight down. The hole in the ice was surrounded by twigs and debris, which had been carefully arranged by the muskrats to keep it from freezing over. Deb Brown admits that she and her fishing partners are much more careful now when ice fishing and hold no ill feelings against the muskrats.

Ontario Alcohol and Boating

Pat Drummond of Manotick, Ontario, spends much of his time researching and documenting various boating statistics and how they relate to safety on the water. On his website BoatinginCanada. com, Drummond looks at alcohol as a cause of drowning while on the water. Pat notes that there

are, on average, 36 boating deaths in Ontario every year and over 30 percent of these are caused by alcohol. The Canadian Medical Association says that alcohol is detected in two thirds of all boating-related drownings where many people are above the legal driving limit.

Fishing-related Drownings

The Lifesaving Society looked at water fatalities between the years 1990 to 1998 and of the water-related deaths in Canada, fishing ranked second, only to swimming. Of the boating accidents involved, 85 percent of drowning victims were not wearing a life jacket or personal flotation device (PFD). It was also discovered that canoes account for 30 percent of all boating fatalities. The province with the highest percentage of households owning watercraft in 1994 was Ontario with 41.3 percent. New Brunswick, Quebec and British Columbia ranked next with between 15 to 18 percent of all households owning a watercraft.

Death by Sinker

A young man from Long Island, New York was fishing at the west end of Jones Beach when he died in perhaps the strangest fishing accident known to man. The three-ounce lead sinker Jaime Chicas was fishing with came out of the water after being snagged on the bottom and struck him in the face. The sinker ripped through his skull and ended up lodged in his brain. Chicas' brother-in-law found him lying on the ground beside his fishing rod with a slight bit of blood dripping from his face. He had no idea what had happened.

After looking at x-rays, doctors at Nassau University Medical Center discovered that the sinker of Chicas' fishing rod had just missed his right eye and entered his head at the bridge of his nose and that the momentum drove the weight across the middle of his brain into the back left side of his head. Officials believe it is the first fishing-related death of its kind ever recorded. Jaime Chicas was only 21 years old.

Chapter Five

Antique Lure Aficionados

Like many other noble pursuits, collecting antique fishing tackle is both a passion and a labor of love for many avid fishermen and women. Unlike some other pastimes, however, collecting antique lures requires a vast knowledge, years of training, a good eye and a dose of luck. For thousands of weird and wacky treasure hunters around the world, the idea of finding that one special addition to their collection or stumbling across a rare lure from days gone by is just the thing to keep them going.

The real fanaticism over antique lures really only came about in the last 20 years or so, and I believe the law of supply and demand was an overriding factor. As with an original oil painting, the age of the work, the artist's name and reputation, as well as the rarity and collectability of the piece are all factors to be considered.

Those folks who call themselves antique lure collectors are among the most dedicated and driven of anyone in the fishing world. One could say that the financial gain of buying and selling antique fishing tackle is only one small part of its appeal. For the diehards of the industry, monetary value is really only a consideration rather than a motivating factor. It is that treasure-hunter instinct and

the excitement of capturing a small part of history that draws people to this pastime. We will hear from some of the most dedicated and famous lure collectors in existence as well as about some of the more remarkable items collected and sold on the market today. Although the United States is the pioneer of vintage lure collecting, Canada has recently followed suit and is now home to some of the more noteworthy examples of historic fishing tackle. Sit back and enjoy this stroll through fishing tackle history.

The "What For and Why"

The reasons behind antique lure collecting are best summed up by world-renowned lure aficionado Dr. Michael Echols. Dr. Echols is considered by many to be one of the foremost authorities in vintage fishing tackle and someone who is extremely knowledgeable of the philosophy behind this pastime. Echols had always been a "hoarder," starting off in his early days with a fine collection of Winchester lever-action rifles. He spent many of his early days searching for these classic weapons and learning more about the financial and market side of a firearms collection. Dr. Echols epitomizes the antique lure aficionado. He has a great interest in preserving the past and loves to travel, to meet new people and to share his interest with others. He also happens to find lure collecting to be a great investment.

For anyone wanting to get into the lure collecting, Dr. Echols emphasizes the need to do copious background research. Start from the ground up, and look for items such as early boxes, as opposed to complete lure sets. Monitoring current lure prices on auction sites like eBay, Echols suggests, is another good way to keep tabs on the market.

Perhaps fishing is, for me, only an excuse to be near rivers. If so, I'm glad I thought of it.

–Roderick L. Haig-Brown, *A River Never Sleeps*

Greenhorn Pointers

Once you have done your research and have a better understanding of the tackle that is of interest to most collectors, begin logging and documenting some of these existing collections. Try to look for interest patterns or areas where people show a great affinity for a certain line of lures. It has been suggested by those in the field that you don't need spend a lot of money on any given fishing tackle unless you feel it to be a good investment for you personally. Put yourself in the mind of other collectors—is that old wooden plug you are looking at something that may appeal to other treasure hunters?

Money is always a factor when starting out. You may have a few extra dollars and want to buy all the old lures that you see right off the bat, but keep in mind that, as with many other antiques, condition is perhaps the most important factor. The same theory holds true for those who collect old Barbie dolls, GI Joe figures and so on. A mint condition GI Joe in the original box is a lot more valuable and desirable than a figure that has been played with. The same goes for vintage fishing lures. Along with condition, according to Dr. Echols, another important aspect of an old lure is the workmanship and complexity. Some of the more complex and extravagant lures of the early days are those with much greater appeal today. Many collectors look for the oddities in a set rather than the run-of-the-mill generic-looking fishing plug.

Try focusing on one specific production year, and again you will see the law of supply and demand come into play. For those dates that are in very low supply, the demand will be high and therefore the item will prove to be a great addition to any collection. Also, keep in mind interest levels and mood changes in the industry. Since tastes and interests fluctuate naturally over time, a once desirable lure may later become a has-been dud and of little value to any collector. One must keep on top of the trends and find out what is hot and what is not.

Did you know?

Fish swimming at depths of 15,000 feet (almost three miles down!) can withstand a pressure of 7000 pounds per square inch. They are able to live at these crushing depths by pumping gas into their swim bladder.

The Holy Grail of Fishing Lures

Any antique lure collector worth his salt will spend many long hours in search of that ultimate prize on which his entire collecting career will be based. As we know, these folks are treasure hunters at heart, continually sifting through many millions of old lures that have fallen through the cracks through the years. It is those needles in the haystack that we forever hear rumors and stories about.

There was one needle in a haystack in 2003 that I will never forget, and it was called the Haskell Minnow. The Haskell Minnow was made by Riley Haskell of Painesville, Ohio, in the 1950s, and this unassuming little fishing lure fetched an incredible $101,200 at an auction on October 11, 2003. The South Carolina construction family who purchased the Holy Grail of fishing lures set a new world record for the highest price ever shelled out for a single fishing collectible. It was during Lang's Sporting Collectibles fall auction at the Roxboro Holiday Inn that the record-setting purchase was made. Tracey Shirley was ecstatic with the acquisition and later said they were willing to go as high as $150,000 for the extremely rare lure.

This special Haskell's minnow was truly a one of a kind and stored in its original box with R. Haskell stamped on one end. Only a dozen or so of any Haskell's minnows have ever turned up in recent years. In 1998, one sold for $22,000 although it was a smaller version of the Haskell Minnow. The Shirley family have now set their own personal goals of acquiring three other sizes of the Haskell Minnows out there, and it is believed that this record will not stand forever.

Record-setting auctions at the Lang auction house are nothing new. Another record was set in the late 1990s when an American-made fishing reel made in 1820 and constructed completely of brass was sold for a whopping $31,350 to George Snyder, a Kentucky watchmaker. Obviously, vintage fishing tackle is big business as the most recent sporting goods auctions grossed an incredible $340,000 when you factor in the buyer's premiums. Many other valuable collectibles that make these auctions are vintage fly-fishing rods and other sporting artwork. There is no doubt that some needles in a haystack can provide huge paydays.

I fish because I love to; because I love the environs where trout are found, which are invariably beautiful…and, finally not because I regard fishing as being so terribly important but because I suspect that so many of the other concerns of men are equally important—and not nearly so much fun.

– Robert Traver, *Anatomy of a Fisherman*

Lure Collecting Addictions

Among his other contributions to the antique lure collecting business, the famous Dr. Michael Echols also diagnosed a problem that runs rampant through the business, but is rarely talked about. It is the dreaded lure-collecting addiction, and much like other addictions such as drugs, alcohol or gambling, it can be severe and debilitating. According to Echols, if you get a craving to buy or find a lure every few days you are probably an addict, if you attend every lure show within several thousand miles of your home, you might be an addict and if you feel like you need "a fix" when you have not found that special lure in quite some time, you are definitely an addict!

Echols goes on to point out that antique lure addictions are, in fact, a serious problem. Perhaps the most serious side effect of a lure addiction is the financial burden it can place on your life and your loved ones lives. If your lure collecting is affecting your daily activity and the way you spend money or budget for your home and daily living expenses, you may have a serious problem. For those rare few with extremely deep pockets who can afford to purchase anything their heart desires, the addiction is not necessarily a serious problem. But if your zest and craving for building more and more display shelves in your rec room starts to affect your personal life, it may be more serious.

Dr. Echols understands the lure-collecting addiction firsthand as he too has taken a walk down that lonely road at one time. His suggestion in dealing with it is to go cold turkey, sell your entire collection and disassociate yourself with each and every person in the antique lure business with whom you once knew. He points out that, much like a drug or alcohol addiction, the only way to get past the urge and control yourself is to cut off all ties and change your way of thinking. Echols suggests that you abandon the addictive material and if you don't, you may go broke and lose your entire family. Although the affliction is serious and may come off sounding tongue-in-cheek, there is some truth to it. I believe those of us with addictive personalities will more easily fall into this trap. The successful antique lure collectors I have researched and spoken with when writing this book were not particularly rich to begin with but were smart in building their collections. Once a certain line or manufacturer of lures has been identified as a target collection, many of the better collectors will sell off mismatched lures from incomplete sets to help finance the purchase of new lures, thereby making their hobby fun and exciting while being a sound financial investment as well. Not all lure collectors have good business sense; this is something that requires development.

Collector Jargon

Collecting vintage fishing tackle, much like collecting any other antique lures, brings with it several buzz words that are unique to the industry. These buzz words make up terminology specific to antique lures and are used, in some cases, to describe the condition of the item and in other cases to describe various parts of the lure. Although the terminology used to describe vintage fishing equipment is somewhat specific to the trade, it can apply to other types of antique grading as well.

One commonly used term used to describe the condition of a vintage lure is "worm burn" which is the result of a plastic worm or bait being left against a lure's paint for an extended period of time. The paint on the lure will melt and a burn like mark similar to that of a cigarette will appear. A worm burn on an antique lure will significantly decrease its value.

"Whizzed" is often used in coin collecting and is also used when describing a vintage lure that has been rubbed or polished extensively beyond the point of practicality. An item that has been "whizzed" will have the outside varnish or finish of the lure partially or completely removed. This too will decrease the value of the antique lure.

Another term is "hangs well." This is the best euphemism for a lure that is really only present-able on one side; in other words, the side that appears outwards away from the wall is nice while the inside may show significant defects.

"Chip" is basically paint loss of varying degrees. "Paint chip" is a term used to describe flaking, scratching and chipping away of paint on the outside of a vintage lure.

A "rub" or a "scrape" when dealing with antique lures is a smooth, shallow or minor paint or varnish loss from rubbing. It is often caused by an abrasion from a large object the lure may have rubbed against.

A "touch up" refers to an item that has been finished up with new varnish or touched up paint as in gill markings. A touch up is frowned upon in this business as it will detract from the lure and therefore render it useless as a collectible. Antique lures are meant to be collected and displayed in their current unaltered, unabridged and unexpurgated condition.

"Pointers" are marks left by lure hooks caused from normal use while fishing. Often they can be minor scratches or tiny punctures in the paint or varnish. Minor pointers or pointers of a slight degree are not that serious.

"Crazing," also called "checking," is a term used in the grading of many old antique items and is basically a minor separation or cracking of the paint or varnish that occurs over time. Crazing is not to be confused with deep splits or cracks in the paint. According to the experts, vintage lures like the Southbend or Heddon, which were heavily varnished in original production, should show natural crazing today and are an indicator of age.

"Hook drag" is another term used to describe the markings left by the lure's hook on the varnish or paint of the bait. The degree of hook drag is relative to the overall condition. If there is only very minor or light hook drag, it may not necessarily detract from the value of the collected lure.

A "beater" is what those in the business call a lure that is in less than average condition and not really suitable for collecting. A beater may be useful as a parts lure; the experts point out that often beaters are stripped down and redone with the help of an artist and occasionally passed off as new lures, but the expert eye can usually tell the difference.

IT'S A FACT

It is illegal to catch a fish in Kansas with your bare hands.

The Buzz on Boxes

As we have learned, the lure box is nearly as important as the lure itself when it comes to a collectible. Since the factory box is often the first thing to deteriorate, it may be one of the most valuable parts of those collections today. A term like "faded lettering" indicates a common problem with lure boxes where the ink has faded from sun and age or maybe even water damage. Sometimes these things are unavoidable unless the boxes have been stored in complete darkness. Insect damage can occur to boxes as well. Because they are made of paper, they are easily damaged by insects.

"Markings" is another term used for lure boxes. Often the original price of the lure is handwritten on the box and may be an interesting indicator as to the value of these baits in the early days.

"Joints" is used for box collectors; since cardboard boxes are overlapped at the corners with paper, they are often the weak points and the first sections to deteriorate. It is suggested that box joints should never be repaired with tape, as this will drastically reduce the value of your collection.

"Water Marked" describes a lure box condition. Watermarks are unusual color changes or marks that appear on the box and are indicative of a box stored in an unstable or damp environment. The extent of water markings is important as they may indicate overall condition of the lure itself. "Dirt Mildew" and "Oil Saturated" are ways to describe soiled boxes or those that show damage from various dirt or debris sources. Some lure boxes may appear old and dingy as a result of dust and mildew while oil can actually saturate a box to the point where it is unrestorable. Collectible lure boxes may also be described as "stiff and hard" (the box corners are square, the sides are straight) versus "mushy and wavy" (the sides will appear wavy as opposed to straight and have a mushy feel as opposed to a stiff or hard feel because of water or moisture damage). Lure collectors, besides being the ultimate nitpickers, are also very descriptive when describing the condition and possible damage sources of their collectibles.

Antique Lure Collecting in Canada

Up until just recently, the rush to covet mass quantities of rare antique lures had been mostly a pastime of those living in the United States. Thanks to organizations like the Canadian Antique Fishing Tackle Association (CAFTA), the popularity of lure collecting in Canada has grown by leaps and bounds. CAFTA is a non-profit organization dedicated to the growth, promotion and development of collecting and preserving our angling heritage. CAFTA and its members recognize the value and importance of lure collecting from the beginner to the world-renowned collector. The organization holds annual trade shows and strives to educate those new to the sport as well as encourages camaraderie among collectors and all those interested in the sport's past. The group produces a regular newsletter and often invites the public to one of their tight-knit yet thoroughly educational trade shows. I can recall a chat I had with a gentleman named Phil McColl of CAFTA several years ago, a fellow who has spent many years building his own collection and who was as free to share as many of his special tips as he felt he could. I thanked Phil for all his information and the images he had sent of some of his favorite lures and, although I was unable to attend the CAFTA seminar that year in Peterborough, Ontario, I do plan on going to one of CAFTA's future events. They seem like a really unique bunch of individuals.

Antique Lures of Ontario

It is staggering to think of the magnitude that old lure companies had and their effect on today's antique lure market. There were dozens of fishing tackle manufacturers located in Ontario alone, based out of anywhere from Toronto to Peterborough, Napanee, Windsor, Perry Sound, Sudbury, Owen Sound, Gravenhurst, Campbellford, Smiths Falls, Walpole Island, Elmira and so on. Some of these manufacturers from the early days were Selco Baits, J. P. Moore, M. Sutton, Bakers Baits, Delorme, Tomlin Bait Company, Colmer Baits, Hotti Tackle and Gardner Mills Skinner, to name a few. Of course, Lucky Strike Bait Works is the province's flagship tackle manufacturer thanks to old Frank Rusty Edgar who still has a hand in the business today. The province of Ontario is known not only for its streams, lakes, wonderful waterways and fishing opportunities, but also for a laundry list of commercial manufacturers and backyard inventors who have called Ontario home. Some of you may actually be fortunate enough to have found old lures manufactured in the province of Ontario. If so, hold on to them.

Fishing …is conducted under continuous tension.

–Arthur Ransome, *Fisherman's Patience,*
Rod and Line

Inside the Mind of One Tackle Collector

Although many folks out there call antique lure collecting their *joie de vivre* and favorite pastime, few people are as dedicated as Andy Clements of Peterborough, Ontario. Andy is a man who has all the required traits of a truly great antique lure collector. He is one of a handful of collectors who is considered a master of his trade. Clements is a retired pro angler and avid lure buff, and I had the opportunity to chat with him about his favorite pastime. "Well, I sort of fell into collecting after a neighbor gave me a dingbat," Andy recalls of his favorite lure by the Creek Chub Bait Company.

After receiving that first dingbat, Clements made it his life's ambition to track down every single dingbat ever produced. At the time, the odd-looking lure cost about $5, and Clements made short work of rounding up every color and configuration he could find of this odd-looking hair bait. After cornering the dingbat market, Clements moved on to some of the other big names in the business. Shakespeare Whirlwinds and Jamison Knights were just some that Andy dedicated himself to acquiring.

Today, Clements boasts some of the most highly prized fishing lures in existence, including the largest collection of 1911 Lockharts known to man. Of course, Clements is a CAFTA member, as is old Bill Edgar, son of Frank Rusty Edgar of Lucky Strike Lures, and Clements confesses that he is forever buying and selling baits and using the money from the ones he sells to purchase new ones that he requires. He calls it reinvesting in the business. Sadly though, for old-timers like Clements, the initial spark for collecting old lures has faded slightly over the years. "Well," Andy says, "I haven't yet found every lure I'm looking for, but I'm getting there." As he nears his golden years sitting in his retirement home in Florida, he does admit that he will one day sell his collection because his son does not share his enthusiasm for antique lures. Andy prefers not to talk about the day that he will have to part with his pride and joy. Like most antique collectors, Andy Clements secretly dreads the day that his collection will have to go to another collector.

Antique Lures and Fishing Itself

As far as intrinsic value goes, antique lures have very little, perhaps only $10–20. There is, however, an emotional connection based on antique lures and other fishing collectibles. It is their worth as historical pieces of art that draws collectors from all over. Most high-end collections are those items that have never actually seen the water or been used in any practical fishing application. These are items that have been put away and stored for 50 to 75 years, kept in pristine condition, with no intention of ever being used to fish with. This begs the question, does antique lure collecting have anything to do with or have any real tie to sportfishing? Some articles and literature out there would have you believe that it does not. I maintain, however, that the collection of antique tackle is so entrenched in the sport of fishing and is so a part of our fishing heritage that it can never be separated. As research indicates, though a grade of lures and other tackle used as an investment tool were not meant to be used for fishing, the craftsmanship that went into the making of said lures had everything to do with the sport. The fact that they are not used for that purpose today has very little to do with the sport. Don't get me wrong, there are just some people out there who love the aesthetic value of old things and there is nothing wrong with that, but I would say the bulk of the diehard historical collectors cannot help but tie in the original purpose of these lures—which is to catch fish—with today's act of establishing large collections of pristine tackle.

The National Fishing Lure Collectors Club (NFLCC)

For those enthusiasts either already involved in the collection of antique lures or wanting to break into this growing pastime, the National Fishing Lure Collectors Club is an organization worth checking out. The NFLCC is a non-profit educational and international organization founded in 1976 as a way to foster awareness of the fishing tackle collecting market both as a hobby and as a way to assist members with their favorite pastime. The NFLCC is a fabulous resource that looks at hands-on ways of identifying and trading antique fishing lures and equipment.

Just as the Canadian Antique Fishing Tackle Association in Canada (CAFTA) does for Canadian enthusiasts, the NFLCC deals with every aspect of the industry, including what's new in the antique lure business, trade secrets and all the inside track on the collection of vintage tackle. The club shares and disseminates information on old rods, reels, catalogs, print material, minnow traps and buckets, as well as antique photos and a wide variety of collectible lures. Being a member of the NFLCC allows one to receive the *NFLCC Gazette* four times a year, keeping them up to date on the comings and goings of the club and industry gossip. The Mansfield, Texas-based organization offers its members limited edition patches and badges as well as back issues of every magazine to keep members up to speed with what is new and what is hot in the industry. I am told that although the NFLCC is American-based, it does have a solid number of Canadian members as well. Included in the *NFLCC Gazette* are sections like "Can you I.D.," various historical articles and a full glossary of photos. The organization's magazine contains many great photos pertinent to antique fishing tackle and articles written by experts in the field and members willing to share their gift and collection information.

Fishing Tackle Museum

The Carl and Beverly White Fishing Tackle Museum is another oddity of antique lures and vintage tackle industry. The museum pays tribute to sportfishing and includes a wide array of historical lures and tackle. It also has on display one of the largest and most comprehensive sportfishing collections and memorabilia in the world.

The museum is committed to fishing and antique tackle and is sponsored heavily by the Oklahoma Department of Wildlife Conservation. While visiting the fishing tackle museum, I suggest a quick stop to get your photo taken with the world's largest lure, another oddity of this already obscure fishing haven. The world's largest lure was donated by a local store that was going out of business, and is now featured as one of over 20,000 pieces on exhibit at the museum.

Carl White, a resident of Oklahoma, is an avid angler and tackle collector who started at a young age. White has said that his curiosity and interest in the crazy crawler—a lure that happened to be the most expensive of its time—led him to the huge collection he has today. From the age of 12, it had also been his dream to open a fishing tackle museum that would include some of his now famous pieces for the world to behold. It would seem that Mr. White's dream has come true. He and his wife, Beverly, purchased many fine fishing artifacts over the years, including a rare Snyder fishing reel at the cost of over $30,000. In 2002, for unknown reasons, White donated his entire collection to the Oklahoma State Aquarium. He now serves as a consultant for *Bassmasters* magazine and is just one strange fact in the world of antique fishing tackle.

*Game fish are too valuable to be caught
only once.*

–Lee Wulff, *Lee Wulff's Handbook of Freshwater Fishing*

The Big Five

One could not discuss vintage lures or the collecting of antique fishing tackle without identifying what I call the big five in the industry. The top five most influential tackle companies are Heddon Fishing Lures, William Shakespeare Company, Creek Chub Bait Company, South Bend Company and the W.J Jamison Company. These lure manufacturers of the early days account for perhaps 80 to 90 percent of all vintage lures bought and sold on the market today. James Heddon and his famous Heddon Lure Company, of course, are at the top of the heap. Heddon was a resident of Dowagiac, Michigan, and an active beekeeper in the late 1800s, with a career in politics and newspaper publishing and the means to launch what would become the most influential lure company North America. Heddon's personal tales of fishing at the Old Mill Pond near his home are legendary, as are the many stories of the hand-carved plugs that bear his name. Heddon, on top of being the most influential of the big five today, was also the first to introduce the top water bait—the Dowagiac casting plug. Although Heddon died in 1911, his sons, Charles and Will, built the company into a family empire and continued to produce top-quality tackle into the 1950s.

William Shakespeare Jr. was often referred to as the Henry Ford of fishing lures. His early tackle was part of North America's founding movement in the use of artificial fishing lures. The first Shakespeare Revolution bait, which came out around 1900, and the Rhodes Wooden Minnow are now some of the most sought-after of the early Shakespeare baits. William Shakespeare Jr. also produced other popular lures such as the Slim Jim Minnow, as well as tackle sold under the Jim Dandy name. Shakespeare lures and tackle continued to be produced well into the 1980s. Collectors also keep an eye out for products made under the Kalamazoo Tackle name, another company acquired by Shakespeare in the early 1900s. According to collectors, some of the early representatives of William's little business are some of most highly prized lures today.

Creek Chubb lures are also some of the most collected tackle in history and, after Heddon, are considered one of the two most sought-after lures in the world. The Creek Chubb Bait Company was founded in 1910 and unlike some of the other early representatives, Creek Chubb made glass-eyed wooden baits and continued using the original materials well into the 1950s. Otherwise known as CCBC, the Creek Chubb lure can be found in almost every tackle box across North America at one time or another. My father and grandfather always had a few in their boxes.

The South Bend Bait Company of Indiana was a business that began as early as 1903 when they patented one of the first wooden minnows. The famous "South Bend Oreno Lures" later appeared around 1915 and were in production until the 1960s. The South Bend early baits, as well as their bait boxes, still catch the eye of lure enthusiasts. The Oreno lure series also included trout versions and those suitable for fly-fishing.

Another influential lure manufacturer in existence and rounding out the top five is the W.J. Jamison Company of Chicago. Mr. W.J. Jamison, or "Smiling Bill" as he was known, was an innovator and pioneer of early baits whose "coaxer lure" has become one of the most famous fishing baits of all time. Jamison started his company in 1904 when he produced a range of effective bass lures and continued for the next decade or so. By 1910, Jamison had decided to market his Coaxer bait and put it to the test. He challenged fellow tackle manufacturer Hans

Decker of New Jersey to a showdown of sorts to see whose lure was superior. The Coaxer came out on top in that challenge, which proved to be one of the most famous fishing duels of the century. The one notable thing about W. J. Jamison lures is how "Smiling Bill" took great care not only in the baits he made but also in the packaging and the boxes he sold them in. Jamison produced a unique box for every lure, and today, there are more than 50 Jamison boxes of different lure styles in existence. Oddly, many collectors today focus strictly on Jamison's unique box design while ignoring the lures altogether.

I suppose when it comes to antiques, there is no accounting for taste. It reminds me of a story my parents told me about one Christmas morning as a child. I had torn off the wrapping paper from that year's most popular toy with such excitement, only to later find more enjoyment with the box it came in. And by virtue of that, I believe there is probably a little kid that dwells inside every antique fishing tackle enthusiast.

Chapter Six

One Day While Out Fishing...

For many people, sportfishing is about spending time on the water with friends and family and hopefully catching a few fish along the way. Oftentimes, though, the best-laid plans don't quite pan out the way you intended. It's a fact; strange things happen while fishing, and occasionally there is a reasonable explanation for that mysterious creature that snapped your line like a twig or that mysterious shadow that appeared from behind a log only to vanish just as quickly. The strange and unexplainable that go along with this sport add a certain sense of *je ne sais quoi* to the sport of fishing. In this section, you will hear tales of staggering creatures and stories of myth and mystery. Thank goodness for the infamous "Fish Tale" we have all heard, as they too play a part in this chapter. The weird and unexplainable, the humorous and downright comical are as essential to the sport as catching fish.

Furry Friend in the Hut

It seems that weather and cold temperatures are not the only strange occurrences during the winter fishing season. Many anglers have reported other strange occurrences while out on the water during the colder months. One such angler is Grant Hopkins of Orleans, Ontario. Grant recalls ice fishing on the Ottawa River around Petrie Island one winter back in the early '90s when two local anglers got the surprise of their lives inside an ice hut. As the two men crouched around an eight-inch hole in the ice slowly jigging their minnow-tipped offering, something strange poked its head out of one of the holes. It was long, black and furry and jumped through the hole, narrowly missing one of the men in the process. Hopkins says "you've never seen two guys move so quick, crashing through the door onto the open ice to escape." The strange visitor ended up being an inquisitive river otter that entered the hut to see what was happening. The furry fur-bearer soon slipped back down the hole and continued on its way downriver in search of food. Apparently the two ice-fishermen sit a little farther back on their chairs these days.

It reminds me of the time I discovered a porcupine living in our camp outhouse. Luckily, I had glanced down the hole before sitting down, or it would have been some serious acupuncture to my buttocks! Its funny, you know, I look down the hole first every time now.

Sea Monster On-board

Steve Hoyland, Jr. and his friends got the surprise of their lives one evening while deep sea fishing in the Gulf of Mexico off the Texas Coast. The men were enjoying a fabulous evening of grouper, snapper and ling cod fishing when all of a sudden, Steve's buddy Bruce got something impressive on the end of his line. Following a 20-minute battle, they hauled up what looked like a prehistoric creature that measured more than six-feet long. The eel-like fish had a mouthful of sharp teeth and was extremely aggressive. As soon as they got a gaff into the large specimen and hauled it aboard, the creature went crazy. It began thrashing around the boat, rearing its head and lunging at the surprised anglers like an anaconda snake. They managed to beat the prehistoric beast down with whatever weapon they used to defend themselves and in all the commotion the almost 100-pound eel fell below to where two more of Steve's buddies were sleeping.

As they turned the light on, they heard the thud of the giant beast; the eel was right by their beds, poised to strike. One of them had a nine-mm pistol and thought perhaps that would be the way to end the struggle. Of course, they were 100 miles from shore and did not want a bullet hole through the boat. As the giant eel slid its way back up onto the main deck, the men took turns beating it with whatever they could find. They tried to knock it down with fire extinguishers, the lid of an ice chest, a gaff and whatever weapon they could get their hands on. Finally, the giant eel was subdued in a blanket and put into the ice chest, but the battle wasn't over. The lid of the ice chest flew open, and the eel slithered out to continue its assault against the men. They were finally able to put down the giant beast and quickly returned to shore; it was an ordeal they all tried to forget. Upon investigation with the local biologist, they discovered their sea creature was an American conger eel, which are extremely rare, but as we have seen are extremely vicious as well. They are a nocturnal predator of the sea with razor sharp teeth and evidently the ability to wreak havoc aboard a fishing boat.

Did you know?

One way to tell the age of a fish is by looking at its scales. They have growth rings just like trees. These are called circuli. Clusters of them are called annuli. Each annuli show one year.

Trout Out of Its Realm

Ron Cutbill of Ottawa is what one would call an oddity magnet. There are just some folks who seem to be always in the right place at the right time, and in Cutbill's case, rare fish and wildlife are drawn to him like a moth to a flame. Two years ago while driving near Perth, Ontario, Ron and his wife spotted what they first thought to be a white-tailed deer. Upon further investigation, the deer suddenly grew a four-foot-long tail and materialized into a large cougar (a beast believed to be extirpated from eastern North America). Then, in the spring of 2008, Ron bettered that freak occurrence by catching, believe it or not, a natural brook trout in the Constance Bay area of the Ottawa River—a river which was always believed to have been devoid of brook trout. That special day, after hauling in a couple of routine hammer-handle pike,

Ron could not believe his eyes when he lifted a bona fide 13.5-inch *Salvelinus fontinalis* from the net. Although there was evidence that a small trout tributary located on the Quebec-side of the river may have been responsible; the chances of a trout making it across to Constance Bay was truly one in a million. Even more amazing was that Ron caught the wayward trout on a floating Rapala lure.

It is the constant—or inconstant—change, the infinite variety in fly-fishing that binds us fast. It is impossible to grow weary of a sport that is never the same on any two days of the year.

– Theodore Gordon (1939)

Slush Bound

Bill Trudeau of Peterborough, Ontario has enjoyed many great fishing trips with his father over the years but there was one trip in the winter of 1982, when Trudeau was only 16 years old, that he would rather forget. He and his dad had heard about some great winter lake trout fishing on Penelope Lake, not far from Sault Ste. Marie, and decided to start up the old snowmobiles and give it a shot. As was the norm with Bill's dad, the two spent the entire day out on the ice, fishing up a storm until it started to grow dark and it was time to leave. The problem was that one of the Ski-Doos would not start, so they made the decision to travel together on Bill's snowmobile back to shore. Unfortunately, it was March, and a thick layer of slush had formed on the surface of the water, causing great difficulty for the snowmobile with two men on it. The Trudeaus decided to pull the snowmobile off to the side and walk to a nearby camp for help and hopefully a Ski-Doo part required to fix his father's machine.

By the time they made it back to shore, after trudging through six to 12 inches of slush, both men were dead tired. Fortunately, the camp owners said they could stay for the night except that they had concerns that the Ski-Doo would freeze into the lake and that they would be stranded for good, so they made the decision to return to the "slushed in" snow machine and lift the track out of the way so that it would not freeze into the lake.

All Bill can remember is how fatigued and scared he was in the pitch black, after dealing with one snow machine and having to return to shore again. His father kept him going with an inspirational kick to the behind once in a while. Bill cannot remember the last time he was that tired and scared and can recall how his dad was his saving grace that day, motivating him to keep on going. The camp owners greeted them when they returned with a fine moose meat dinner and warm beds for the night. The two were able to return later to fix the broken down snowmobile and rescue the one partially frozen in the lake. Experiences like these, although not the most positive ones, sometimes form the strongest bonds between father and son. Bill recounted the story to his dad one evening many years later at a hunt camp when his father had suffered an aneurysm. Bill reminded his dad of how he had been so strong for him on that evening in 1982, and that it was his turn this time.

Cheetah Power Bath

Each spring since 1989, my father, brothers-in-law and I have gone on a fishing trip into Northern Quebec. It is a special time of camping in the wilderness and sharing many unique traditions—some of which our own families are not even aware. For example, the boys and I maintain a trip diary called a tome, and we award prizes each year for the coveted M.E.R. Cup, with each letter representing our last names. The winner of this fine trophy is the fisherman/camper who has exhibited not only fine angling skills by catching lots of fish, but who has done his share around camp and shown a positive spirit throughout the trip. I am proud to say

I'm a seven-time M.E.R Cup Champion, an achievement I have never bragged about, not because I'm not proud, but because no one would know what the heck I was talking about!

After 20 years of traditions like this, I'd say we all know each other quite well. But what Steve, Bruce and my dad don't realize is that I have another little tradition of my own that no one in the world knows about—well, until now anyway. During the trip, we usually take on different roles around camp: mine is one of gadget, gimmick and supply guy since I always have a cornucopia of fishing equipment and other tools with me at any given time. What can I say? I'm into that sort of thing! Well, about four years back I started bringing along a new gimmick with me—a somewhat obscure beverage called Cheetah Power Surge. I happen to love this power drink produced out of Brantford, Ontario, and the boys love nothing more than teasing me about it. What they didn't realize, though, was my secret trick involving Cheetah.

Not only do I enjoy drinking this caffeine-free nectar of the Gods, but I have been secretly sharing it with our bait each morning before we head out, in a sort of Cheetah bath, you might say. After breakfast when no one was looking, I'd pull our earthworms out of the can one by one and dip them ever so gently into a small glass of bubbling Cheetah.

"There, that should liven them up a little," I thought. Wow! Those night crawlers would jump to attention when they hit the Cheetah! And the look on their little faces was priceless. If only worms could talk! Then, after soaking all the worms in their new "power juice," I'd surreptitiously return them to their sphagnum moss nesting material recharged, rejuvenated and ready to catch fish!

On our last trip north, I must say we really did cash in on the trout too, and the boys had no idea why! It was one of our best years on record for both quality and quantity. Bruce caught his largest Quebec red trout ever—a big 21-inch male around five pounds, and Steve got his picture smack dab on the front cover of *Outdoor Sportsman* magazine holding another big "Cheetah" trout we landed that week. As strange as it may sound, I truly believe the Cheetah power bath had something to do with it, and for what it's worth, you can bet I'll be dipping my bait again next spring! See, I told you fishermen were somewhat odd.

Record Catfish Simply Child's Play

Most anglers these days pride themselves on using the latest and greatest fishing equipment. Extravagant fishing equipment is becoming the rule rather than the exception, and the more it costs seems all the better. But do you need all the fancy bells and whistles to catch big fish?

Not really, as proven by David Hayes of Wilkes County, North Carolina.

David and his granddaughter Alyssa were having a ball fishing for a bluegill in a private pond near their home when young Alyssa decided she had to go to the bathroom. David held Alyssa's hot pink Barbie fishing rod as his granddaughter answered her call of nature.

Within minutes of Alyssa leaving, the bobber disappeared and a swirl could be seen near the surface. David had a fish on, but this was no bluegill! He knew right away the 30-inch child's fishing rod would likely not hold such a large fish, so he battled it out the best he could, going easy on the rod.

After fighting the fish for over 25 minutes, the behemoth specimen made its way to shore. When Hayes hoisted the fish ashore, he could not believe his eyes. It was a monster 21-pound, 1-ounce channel catfish with an incredible 22.5-inch girth, and a length greater than that of the Barbie rod he caught it on.

David Hayes' giant catfish was weighed on certified scales and witnessed by a fisheries biologist with the Wildlife Resource Commission. The catfish was the largest ever caught in North Carolina, beating the old state record by nearly three pounds. So, who says you can't catch big fish on less than impressive tackle? I bet Hayes' granddaughter wishes now she hadn't gone to the bathroom!

Bebee's Tallest Fish Tale

Ed Bebee, on top of being an avid angler and active member of the Ottawa Fishing Club, happens to be one damn fine writer as well. In Ed's second book, *Pathfinders: the Guides of the Rideau,* he recounts the story of a famous valley fishing guide, George Carr, and the man's ability to weave perhaps some of the tallest fishing tales known to man. Here is a classic Ed writes about in his book:

> George Carr was one of the old guides at Portland back in the '50s. He had started guiding some time after World War I. He loved the tourists and they loved him. He would beguile them with the same stories, year after year. George would put on a drawl —a complete act.

> George guided out of Babcock's fishing camp. In the morning, he and the other guides would be hanging around Dowsett's at the marina. He'd wait until he had a good-sized audience before he launched one of his tales about lake trout fishing. One of them went something like this:

> Years ago, I was guiding a party from Pennsylvania—a right big man. We was fishing lake trout, of course. The fishin' had been good that time, and I felt cocky. I told that gentleman that we might be lucky.

The wind was a bit fresh, but no problem for someone like me. I'd been fishing here a long time, yessir, and I knew how to row. Yessir, and I knew where to fish.

George would pause, scowl at the other guides and then turn and wink at his audience.

If you've ever heard anything different from these other guys, well, sir, I showed them where to fish. If they know anything, they got it from me. Anyway, as I say, we were rowing along and we were passing Bass Bay headin' for Tar Island.

All on a sudden, my party yelled that he had a fish! Well, I hope to tell you he had a good one. After about 30 minutes, we got that trout up along the boat. I gaffed it smartly and dragged it in. I reckon that it was about 30 pounds. Real nice fish.

Well, sir, he pulled out a flask and we took a few pulls on it just to steady ourselves.

I touched up the hooks on his Johnny Green spoon—them old trout have tough mouths.

Did I say that I never use nothin' but a Johnny Green spoon and a big green sunfish tail?

By now, even the ones who heard this story last year are listening intently.

As I was tellin' ya, by this time, we was near Tar Island, so we turned around and started rowing back west towards Trout Island. We'd got back in front of Horseshoe Bay when my party let out a yelp and said that he had a real strong one on this time.

Well, for a big man, he was always a little excitable and I figgered he was still a bit high after the big fish he'd just caught. But that rod of his had a right good bend in it. After twenty minutes or so, he was starting to puff pretty hard, so I decided to give him a breather. Told him to take another suck on his flask, calm his nerves, y'know.

I took the rod and started crankin' real hard and pumped the rod and that fish started comin' up. I knew it was a good one, I could feel the throb in that steel line.

After ten minutes or so, my party had his wind back and I gave him the rod.

George paused here to survey the audience. A few more men and a young boy had joined the crowd. He continued:

I told him to start really pushing that fish—just crank and pump, crank and pump—you know what I mean, if you've ever had the luck to fish with me. Pretty soon we had that fish up and wallerin' on the surface, a ways out from the boat.

Boys, I tell ya, it was the biggest damn trout I ever seen! It looked like a cow out there, but longer.

Anyway, not to make a big story outta it, we pulled up along side and I said to my party," Now, then, when I get the gaff into it, and start pullin' him aboard, you try and grab him down by the tail and lift!" We done it—we rolled that fish over the side of that old green Dowsett skiff and my party sat on it.

He took out his flask and we had quite a few pulls on it this time.

George stopped, a faraway look in his eyes, remembering that big trout, or maybe the flask.

What'd ya say there, sonny? How big was it? Well, to tell the God's honest truth, I dunno. But mebbe some these educated fellows here can figger it out, if I say that when we got that there fish into the boat, it took a good five minutes for that hole to fill back up with water!"

Now George had his audience eating out of his hand. George always found a new wrinkle to freshen up an old story.

With enthusiastic encouragement, George would start his next story:

Well, sir, I was out trolling along the North Shore there and I'd been at it for a few hours. I was on the circuit—down to Trout Island and loop around and row all the way back up past Bass Bay to Tar Island.

Now, I was using steel line and a Johnny Green spoon with a green sunfish tail on it—yessir, can't be beat, if you're looking for big fish. Mind you have sharp hooks and touch them up if you happen to bounce them off the stones.

Anyway, as I say, I was rowing along, and suddenly, I seen the rod tip bounce—once, twice, three times—and then bend right over. Yessir, I knew that I was into a good 'un.

I set the hook smartly—I was young and strong then, a man in full, if you catch my meaning. I knew that the fish was mine—just a matter of time. I started to crank on that old Penn reel.

Well, sir, after twenty minutes or so, I began to think that maybe this wasn't going to be so easy. I hadn't gained but a few yards of that steel line and most of the time it was twanging like a cheap guitar.

George would pause here and look around the crowd. They were spellbound.

Well, I started to think about how this was going to end. How was I going to get this fish?

Well, there wasn't any help for it—I didn't see nobody I knew. All I could do was keep crankin' and hope I could wear him out before it wore me down.

I kept gaining line slowly and it looked like it might be winning. Suddenly that fish just turned and went down like a rock—couldn't stop it, nossir!

Anyway, I started cranking again and I began to think about going for help. Well, sir, I was close to Trout Island, you can't see it from here, it's right out there to the west—about 4 miles or so. The fish was quiet and not taking line, so I set the rod down, clicker on, drag set, and started to row.

I had the rod over the side, and my big size 11 boot planted on the handle. If I take it easy, I figured to make it to Trout Island in about 10 minutes. Pretty soon I was getting close to a little island just south of Baby Trout Island.

A few minutes more and I'm beaching the boat on that little island, with that fish still swimmin' out there at the end of that steel line. I got outta the boat real careful, picked up the rod and walked slowly up to a stout tree, about 4 inches across, I guess. I quickly took a couple of turns around the tree to make sure that the line wasn't gonna slip.

Yessir, I was feeling pretty pleased with myself when I got back into the boat and started to lather the water towards the bungalow. When I got there, Will Ripley was just coming in. I shouted at him to follow me and we set out for that little island.

Well, sir, when we got back, not 20 minutes after I'd tethered that fish, Will and I just sat there and stared at each other.

Nossir, you won't believe this, but the island was gone! Baby Trout was still there—you can go out and check for yourself, but that little one was gone. That damned fish just dragged it off into deep water!

George would shake his head in bewilderment, and put on a hangdog look, shoulders slumped.

He went on in a low, solemn voice.

Will found the little island a few days later. He was trolling up through that deep slot here between Trout and Long Island.

Well, sir, he hit a new reef with his lines and Will, he dragged up my old outfit.

Believe it or don't!

(Reprinted with permission from Ed Bebee)

Uninvited Guest

Glenn Dobby of Toronto is no stranger to the fishing world because his father, Jerry, brought him up on the ways of the water and how to understand nature. One day, while boating with his girlfriend at his cottage near Burleigh Falls, Glenn witnessed something he had never seen in all his years on the water. As they sat in their 18-foot cruiser on Labor Day weekend of 2009 watching the sun go down, the two were about to fire up the boat and head back to the cottage when they were startled by a thumping sound on the side of the boat. Without warning a huge snake, in the four to five foot range and as thick around as a pop bottle, slithered into the boat and coiled up on the rear bench seat. Neither of them had seen such a large snake before, especially at such close proximity. "What do we do now," they pondered, as Glenn reached for a paddle he had in a storage compartment while keeping a watchful eye on the creature that had taken up residence in the boat.

Just as he reached with the paddle to lift the giant snake back in the water, the beast reared its head and slipped backed over the side as quickly as it came. After returning to the cottage and sharing his story, I did some research and discovered that Glenn's monster was actually a northern water snake—a non-poisonous resident of the Northern United States and Canada and,

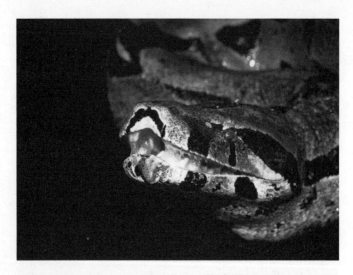

although they are rare, do not pose a threat to human life. It is believed, though, that the northern water snake will bite if picked up, so it was a good thing that Mr. Dobby didn't try to do that. I don't believe that either of them have since returned to that part of the lake.

IT'S A FACT

In Muncie, Indiana it's a crime to carry fishing tackle into a cemetery.

Just Noodling Around

Noodling is a strange fishing technique carried out in parts of the Southern United States and one we will learn more about in the next chapter. The angler, or "noodler," is immersed in the water and uses his or her hands and fingers as bait to catch giant catfish. The idea is to entice catfish into chomping down on your hand, so that you may—hopefully—wrestle them to the surface. The problem here is the size and strength of these giant cats; oftentimes the angler gets pulled under the water and drowns, or is swept away in a high current as did one Oklahoma noodler in 2008. Although the statistics are sketchy, there appears to have been perhaps a dozen or so noodling deaths reported over the years, making this weird and wacky sport not one for the faint of heart.

Filmmaker Bradley Beesley brought this strange subculture to the surface, so to speak, in a movie he made about hand fishing called *Okie Noodling*. Beesley's motto for the sport is "no worms, no wimps and no worries," which seems to somewhat aptly sum up this very odd American tradition. So far, hand fishing for catfish is legal in 11 states and is usually carried out only in shallow water, although some of the more brazen noodlers do it in water that's neck-deep. Other dangers of noodling, of course, are the creatures one might find in a catfish hole such as alligators and snakes.

In a sport where anglers use their own bodies as bait, they have a high risk of being bitten by any number of creatures or pulled to their deaths by a giant fish. I'd say these folks are more than just noodling around. It may be weird and slightly disturbed, but it is a fact of fishing today.

Over-aggressive Lunge

Chris Pepper was muskie fishing one day on the Ottawa River near Rockland when he gained a newfound respect for nature's boldest fish. Chris was moving down the river shoreline, casting to a weed flat that broke into a deep water drop-off, when all of a sudden he saw a large muskie chasing his lure to the boat. Following closely behind a lure without striking is a behavior these fish are notorious for. It was a large lunge, too, in the 50-inch range and after the follow, she quietly disappeared under the boat. Chris went into his muskie "figure 8," a technique that will often trigger a strike; however, it did not work this time. Moments later, while standing on the bow of the boat chatting with his partner about the brief nuclear sub encounter, they heard a loud BANG!! He thought he had hit bottom with the electric trolling motor.

Chris glanced at the fish finder, which displayed 20 feet, and then looked over the side of the boat to see what he had banged into, and there she was swimming down and away from the trolling motor propeller. The big muskie that followed

Chris' lure had actually attacked his bow-mount electric trolling motor! Pepper could not believe what had just happened, since he runs an extremely powerful 74-pound thrust 24V MinnKota Maxxum. The poor fish must have developed an instant migraine after having a mouthful of steel and composite plastic. Chris figured the big muskie must have waited under the boat after following his lure, and the slowly spinning propeller must have driven her nuts until she snapped and couldn't resist any longer. Chris and his fishing partner joked that perhaps they would need a bigger boat next time. Although it is a rare phenomenon, I discovered that this sort of attack has happened to other fishermen over the years. Those muskellunge are bold fish indeed!

Fear of Water

David Batty of Orleans, Ontario, will never forget the summer of 1977 and his first trip to Mistassini—Quebec's largest and most famous lake. Batty was a keen fisherman, although he had a definite distaste for water and a fear of drowning. Unfortunately, Quebec's 150-mile long Mistassini Lake has a tendency to get rough because of its long, narrow configuration as well as it being fairly shallow in areas. On a windy day across the main lake, waves can reach the four to five foot range, which is exactly what happened on Mr. Batty's first trip to Mistassini. As they left the sheltered confines of Peniquion Bay inlet, Dave had no idea of the rough water he was about to encounter. The men did their best to keep the boat pointed toward their island destination some 50 miles up the lake, but the pounding waves had other ideas.

With two young boys on board, it was everything Batty and his partner could do to keep the outboard going and the boat properly "planed out."

"The water was coming in big time and I was sure scared," Batty recalls. "But when I was told to pull the plug on the boat and that we had enough speed to drain some water out, I went from scared to petrified!" Batty was not a strong swimmer to begin with, and since ice out on Mistassini had only been two weeks previous, he knew the 40°F water would create an instant tomb for anyone who fell in. For the next two hours, Dave bailed and kept his wits about him as they bobbed like a cork out on mighty Lake Mistassini. Finally, the weather died down, and the men managed to creep their way up to the island where they were to camp. Dave did return to Mistassini again following that trip but, fortunately, never encountered the waves the way he did that day. He does not know how close they came to capsizing in their extremely weighted down 16-foot utility boat. That is something he would rather not think about.

Peculiar Pike

One evening in 1994, while I was out fishing with Diederic Godin of Edmonton on Quebec's Bevin Lake, I witnessed something I still have no explanation for. Diederic and I had planned a nice, quiet evening of walleye fishing on our favorite lake in the Laurentian Mountains and were going through our tackle selection as we cruised up Bevin Lake's western shore. Out of the corner of his eye, Diederic noticed some movement on the lake surface about 200 yards from shore. As we slowed down and approached the object, we could not believe our eyes. It was a northern pike of perhaps five to seven pounds swimming with its head completely out of the water. It was as if the fish was breathing in air to inflate its swim bladder, but of course, we knew that pike do not do such a thing.

The peculiar pike continued moving around the lake with its head out of the water for several minutes, swimming in circles, occasionally dipping below the surface and then plunging its snout six to eight inches back out of the water. Neither of us could believe what we were witnessing. "This is like something out of the Twilight Zone," Diederic commented. I agreed and as the strange fish slowly returned to the depths of Bevin Lake, we were left scratching our heads. My background in fisheries biology provided no answers for this phenomenon. As we have seen, though, the strange and unexplained oftentimes accompany this sport, which sure does make things interesting.

...you must endure worse luck sometime,
or you will never make a good angler.

–Izaak Walton, *The Compleat Angler*

Casting for Interns

Contrary to popular belief, not all fishing takes place on the water. In April 1996, classic rock radio station CHEZ 106 in Ottawa held the first annual "Casting for Interns" competition as a way of ushering in the spring and providing some PR for the annual sports and cottage show that was about to hit town. This fishing challenge pitted famous Canadian Angler Big Jim McLaughlin against the *Ottawa Sun* Outdoors Guy (yours truly) in a competition like no other. Live on the *Doc and Woody* radio show, Eric the intern—dressed up as a freshwater fish—was the target in the stunt held on the grounds of the CHEZ 106 property. Both Big Jim and the Outdoors Guy were equipped with fishing tackle and real live casting plugs. Big Jim, being the seasoned bass fishing veteran, opted for a bait casting outfit while the Outdoors Guy went with the ever-popular spinning rod.

Well, this fishing trip was not your normal adventure at all. Big Jim and the Outdoors Guy took turns casting and trying to hook Eric the intern as he swam along the grass in front of the CHEZ studios. After 10 minutes of casts, some near misses and some direct hits, Big Jim McLaughlin, as was expected, was deemed the winner of the first and last annual casting for interns competition. As a footnote, the casting for interns fishing challenge was the third annual challenge between the Outdoors Guy and Big Jim McLaughlin. Previous years included a trivia competition with fishing and hunting questions for each of the competitors live an on the air. The big winner in all this was, of course, the Ottawa Sportsman Show for all the exposure it was given. Additionally, it was a fabulous way to usher in the springtime.

If fishing interferes with your business, give up your business…the trout do not rise in Greenwood Cemetery.

–Sparse Grey Hackle, *"Murder" Fishless Days*

Two Trout for the Price of One

Steve Enright, besides being my brother-in-law, happens to be one of the luckiest trout anglers I've ever seen. In the 20-some years I have been fishing with Steve up north, he has always been in the running for the "most fish" award. I can recall one particular year, though, that he took his trout-catching prowess to a whole other level. As Steve and I rowed the old Sportspal canoe around one of our favorite trout lakes, I watched as he set the hook on yet another spunky brook trout—third one in a row—only this time the fight that ensued felt a bit different, Steve claimed. "It's like my line is going in two different directions," he said as it neared the side of the canoe. As I dipped my landing net to scoop out his trout, we soon discovered why his line had been moving in two different directions. On the end of Steve's line was not one, but two nice-sized brook trout, both caught on the same hook!

Now I had heard stories about two fish being caught on a single hook, but most times it involved a treble—a hook with three separate barbs on it. This time, however, Steve managed to hook and hold two separate trout with a single hook and land them both safely. The number six snelled hook he used on that particular lake was small enough so that when the first trout hit Steve's line it became hooked and since we use worms as bait, a second

trout had evidently come along and pulled the worm out of the first one's mouth. Apparently, in doing so, the second fish managed to get himself caught, while sliding trout number one up the line, yet still firmly attached. It would be sort of like threading a needle twice, I would imagine. Well, the odd two-for-one deal occurred back in May 2002, but is a story we often talk about when we get together. In fact, Steve has yet to stop bragging about it!

Tale of the Sinking Ice Hut

In January 2007, Pierre Menard and his dad, Rolland, spent a week ice fishing on scenic Lake Nippissing when Mother Nature threw them a major curveball. During their last night on the lake, camped out in an ice hut, the temperature rose to 52°F, and they experienced a wicked thunderstorm. The next morning when they

woke up and looked outside, there was no more snow left on the ice, and all they could see for miles was water! The men thought for sure their ice hut was sinking. Pierre immediately ran outside, took out his ice pick out and checked the depth. "Pheeef, there's still 30 inches of ice out there, Dad," he declared with a sigh of relief.

When the snowmobile arrived, with an attached transport "chuck wagon," to pick them up, the men proceeded to shore about one and a half miles away. Menard will never forget looking through the back window of the chuck wagon, and all he could see were waves created by the snowmobile. "It was so weird," Pierre recalls. "It felt like being in a boat but we were on ice, a very strange feeling indeed."

Menard's father passed away from prostate cancer shortly after that trip. Pierre looks back on the many fishing adventures he spent with his dad over the years. Through thick and thin, the Menard boys managed to tackle more water and more fish than most of us have ever seen. I'm sure the loss of a close friend and fishing companion is something one never completely gets over, especially when it's your father.

I know literally thousands of fishermen, yet in all this multitude I can number only four men who can handle a bass fly rod the way it should be handled...

–John Alden Knight, *Black Bass*

Chapter Seven

Fishing Methods & Techniques

The ancient art and practice of catching fish dates back nearly 40,000 years. There is, in fact, an isotope analysis of a 40,000-year-old human from Asia that shows consumption of freshwater fish. The ancient art of fishing has become a way of life for people around the world and dozens of different techniques and fishing strategies have developed over time. In the early days of fishing, very primitive techniques were employed because of such limited resources at the time, but with the progression of man and evolution, the once-crude techniques for catching fish slowly increased in complexity and effectiveness.

A wide variety of proven fish catching strategies are used today in both sport and commercial fishing industries. There are also some more obscure techniques used by anglers of different cultures, and everyday tactics used by folks on a daily basis. Most fish catching techniques are viewed as

ethical and fair, while others, like blasting and poisoning, have been deemed not only politically incorrect but also cruel. And, what may seem odd to us here in North America is second nature to others. The ability of man to catch fish is a basic cornerstone of our heritage, and in this chapter we will explore and understand the origins of how modern man learned to catch fish, and we will also see the many different recreational and commercial fishing techniques that exist around the world. Some are conventional while others are a bit more off the beaten track. They are all, nonetheless, a fact of this great activity we call fishing.

Subsistence Fishing

The act of subsistence fishing implies the various techniques used to catch fish for personal consumption in order to live. Subsistence fishing is quite different than the sportfishing of today, as it usually does not carry all the "bells and whistles";

however, it does share some common similarities. North American Aboriginal people have relied heavily on subsistence fishing with the use of various techniques, including spears, harpoons, hand lines and different netting techniques. Since subsistence fishing continues today in various communities, the control over the equipment used is practically non-existent. Communities around the world that still catch fish for their own consumption will oftentimes use equipment that may be viewed as primitive by today's standards, yet is still extremely effective at putting fish on the table.

Gill Netting

A gill net is a long, nylon woven mesh net suspended in the water column with the idea of capturing any fish that gets tangled in it. The size of the fish captured is governed by the size of the mesh on the gill net. Native fishing communities still use gill nets in the far North regions. These nylon mesh gill nets are stretched over a long distance anywhere from shallow to open, deeper water. Any fish species large enough to get caught in the net's mesh will force themselves through, causing their gills and gill plates to become stuck and keeping them from getting out. The gill nets are highly effective at catching fish; however, they are quite indiscriminate in the species that they catch. Ducks, loons and other waterfowl, amphibians and reptiles may also

become entangled in a gill net quite easily. So, as effective as the gill net is, the fact is they can also be deadly to many non-target fish species and other wildlife.

He had been hooked two or three times and was consequently wary as a miser, when his son begins to beat about the bush, introductory to some pecuniary hint.

–Hewitt Wheatly, *The Rod and Line*

Hand Fishing

Hand fishing, or noodling, as it is called throughout much of the Southern United States, is one fishing technique, as strange as it is, that seems to have developed an almost cult following. Hand fishing is a technique usually done to catch catfish, whereby anglers fully immerse themselves in the water, oftentimes with a diving suit, and feel around with their hands in a lake or river for bottom-dwelling catfish. Once the location of a catfish is identified, the angler then reaches inside the big cat's mouth and begins hauling the fish to the surface. In some southern areas of Arkansas, Texas and Georgia where large blunt-head catfish are found, people hand fish with great success and have pulled in some very large fish, sometimes weighing more than 50 pounds.

An experienced hand fisher will often feel around the mud and stumps of a river bottom first, before diving down and grabbing with their hands. The equipment required to hand fish is very basic. One needs a good pair of hands, a strong swimming ability and very little clothing so as not to get lodged on any underwater obstructions during a hand fishing session. I assume they would also require a fair amount of nerve. There are photographs all over the Internet now of giant catfish pulled in by hand fishing or noodling. I suppose one plus side to the sport is never having to worry about access to bait, since none is required.

Cormorant Fishing

The use of other wildlife to help catch fish is not something one readily sees in any parts of North America, but in Asia it is quite common. Anglers on the Li and Yangtze rivers in China, for example, employ an odd technique for catching fish, which involves the use of cormorants. These large fish-eating birds can swim underwater at great speeds for long distances, and catching fish is what they do to survive. Quick-thinking residents of the region have learned how to tame these birds, putting the cormorant's fish-catching ability to work. Anglers float out on bamboo rafts with their cormorant friends tucked under their arms, ready to get fishing. Each cormorant is set out in the river and trained to return to the raft once it has a fish in its mouth. In the beginning, the cormorant must have a string fastened around its gullet so that it cannot swallow the fish it catches. After a while, some well-trained cormorants don't even require a "neck noose" and learn not to swallow the fish. Asian anglers who use these birds are known to take very good care of them and always make sure to feed them properly. Maintaining the health of your feathered meal ticket, I can see being of the utmost importance.

Fly-fishers fail in preparing their bait so as to make it alluring in the right quarter, for want of a due acquaintance with the subjectivity of fishes.

–George Eliot, *The Mill on the Floss*

Drift Netting

Drift netting is a technique that has been used by commercial fisheries on the high seas for many years. It is a technique whereby huge nets—sometimes more than half a mile in length—are set out on open water and allowed to drift freely, capturing everything in their path. A large-scale drift netting program for swordfish and tuna was banned in 2002 because of its effect on striped dolphin. The deadly drift nets have no control over what gets caught in them. Very little drift netting goes on today as the environmental impact of this technique is so great. Marine entanglement has fortunately become a high-profile issue that even salmon and tuna sold on the market today are marketed as drift net-free fish. It is an effective technique for catching a wide variety of fish species, but again, the number of incidental catches is staggering.

Fishing with Otters

It may be hard for us in North America to fathom, but river otters are also used in different areas of the world to help catch fish. In parts of India, Sri Lanka and Scandinavia, otters are trained to swim around in circles to scare fish into nets. Since otters are famous fish feeders, their mere presence in the water causes schools of fish to move from one place to another, and fishers have learned to use this behavior to their advantage. Strange, but true.

Did you know?

The stonefish, which lives off the coast of Australia, is the most poisonous fish in the world.

Aquaculture

The farming of fish of different species in a hatchery setting is an extremely important fisheries management tool. In North America, fish species, such as several species of salmon and trout, are farmed in a hatchery environment today. Fish aquaculture involves the artificial or human reproduction and hand spawning of a given fish species. The hatchery-produced fish are raised in a captive setting and often used for supplemental stocking. With the pressures of recreational fishing in North America today, supplemental fish stocking is a must. Hatchery or farmed fish are frequently introduced into native or non-native waters with the idea of mixing with natural fish stocks and complementing the overall ecosystem. Other fish farms include the production of fish for fishmeal, including species such as carp and goldfish. There are dangers associated with fish farming and aquaculture, given the species raised in the hatchery environment control, and proper aquaculture techniques are required at all times. Fish farming and the domestic raising of fish stocks should be carried out by trained biologists.

Trammel Netting

A trammel net is similar to a gill net, although it is divided into three separate layers of netting. It is an inner fine mesh layer sandwiched between two outer mesh nets. The net is then secured at the base, allowing it to hang vertically. This kind of net is effective for commercial fisheries but, as with drift netting, the dolphin-friendliness of the fishing equipment is a consideration. Some of the more modern fishers now attach acoustic devices called "pingers" to their equipment as a way of keeping dolphins and porpoises away from the nets. The pingers produce a loud, aggravating sound wave that helps these animals steer clear of the nets. Of course, the decisions made by the commercial fishers will often make or break the success of their equipment. A thorough understanding of the waters they are fishing is also essential, as is the length of time these nets are left to soak.

Stalking along from log to log, or plunging their long legs in the oozy swamp, the two herons paid no attention to my presence, but occupied themselves with their own fishing arrange-ments, as if their wilderness were their own.

–W.C. Prime, *I Go A-Fishing*

Hand lining

Hand lining is one of the oldest fishing techniques in existence. It involves a coiled up spool of line,

a hook, some bait and a weight. Hand lining is quite popular in areas where vertical jigging is the only option available. Hand lining for cod, mackerel and squid is an effective method of catching these fish. I will never forget the time I went hand lining for cod years ago off Seal Cove, Newfoundland. It felt so foreign to be fishing without a rod and reel, but when I felt the tug of large cod at the end of my line, it was great fun pulling it in. A lot of hand lining in the Maritimes is done the old fashioned way as the name implies. Some techniques now include the use of a hydraulic or electric line retrieval device. With the more modern hand-lining devices, several members of the crew may get involved while on board and since some fish species are caught at great depths, a manual retrieval of line is quite labor intensive and puts a fair strain on the person at the other end.

...there are enough miles of bright water in the Blue Ridge to support the fly fisherman's deep-seated need to believe in infinite possibilities.

–Christopher Camuto, *A Fly Fisherman's Blue Ridge*

Jigging

Jigging is also a very old technique for catching fish and is often done vertically at boat side, but it can also be carried out effectively from shore or on a slow drift. Fishing jigs vary greatly in size, weight and configuration. Jigging is the most common way of winter fishing where jigs are often tipped with minnows, worms or leeches as bait. It has become an effective method of angling for recreational fisher men and women in that the jig and bait may be presented in a zone closer to where the fish are hanging out. Jig users find that they are even able to attract inactive fish by presenting their jig vertically within the fish's strike zone. Other methods of fishing often require the fish to be actively feeding in order to strike. Jigs are usually composed of a lead belly, a lead base or a lead head molded to a hook and then dressed with a twist or tail, a skirt or some other type of attracting hair. Most anglers will work the jig with a snap of the line and then allow it to flutter down slowly.

Trap Netting

Trap netting is another widely used fishing technique in which large nets are anchored to the bottom of the body of water. This method includes a large trap holding area and long wings that extend out perpendicular to the trap. These long, small, mesh wings act as deflectors to angle the fish back to the holding area of the net. Any fish that swim along the bottom and hit a wing deflector will follow the length of that net to the trap opening, which is angled inwards much like a minnow trap, thereby enclosing the fish in the trap area. Trap netting is used in different parts of the world, frequently to catch salmon, and also by various fisheries managers as a safe way of trapping fish for sampling purposes. Trap nets have a hatch on the top of the section where the trapped fish are kept so they can be netted, pulled out live and later released back into the water. Most trap nets are made of heavy mesh and the fish do not actually become tangled in the net in any way. It is a relatively safe and humane fishing method often used by trained professionals to catch fish that will be later live released.

IT'S A FACT

In Montana, it's illegal for married women to go fishing alone on Sundays, and illegal for unmarried women to fish alone at all. It is also against the law for a man to knit during fishing season.

Dynamite or Blast Fishing

This extremely dangerous method of catching fish has been prohibited in most areas of the world. It is a simple but brutal technique where an explosive device—such as dynamite—is detonated in the water, sending a shockwave that kills all fish in a large radius. Since explosive or blast fishing is extremely deadly, it often kills other sea creatures, including fragile coral reef, in the process. In such countries as the Philippines, the practice of blast fishing has continued to some extent and unfortunately, even though it has been outlawed in most areas in recent years, many fragile coral reefs in Southeast Asia have already been destroyed by explosive fishing.

Trolling

Trolling is an extremely popular technique in sportfishing today. It is similar to the trawler methods used in the commercial industry, and for the sportfishing enthusiast, trolling can be a way of life. On much of the Great Lakes, where a sheer amount of water and extreme depths are present, trolling with the use of down rigging equipment is the only technique used. Trolling occurs when a bait lure is run behind a boat under the power of the boat. Trolling can be done while paddling a canoe, rowing a rowboat, motoring in a motorboat or using an electric trolling motor. Trolling is popular simply because of its ease of use and the opportunity to cover a lot of water. Anglers often use trolling to locate active fish with the use of a sonar or fish finder and may switch to other techniques once a trolling pass has produced a strike or two. In the early season when many fish are running shallow, trollers sometimes use equipment like planer boards to take their bait away from the boat as the spooked fish tend to shy away from the sound of a motor boat in shallow water. Trolling is one of the most popular fish-catching techniques used in freshwater fishing today.

Dive Fishing

Dive fishing is a type of fishing carried out by either a diver equipped with an underwater diving tank setup or a skin diver with a mask, snorkel and flippers. Dive fishing is usually carried out with a spear or a spear gun. Dive anglers travel below the surface spotting and stalking their underwater fish in the hopes of either spearing it with a hand spear or shooting it with a spear gun. Dive fishing is still carried out today in areas of the South Pacific and small pockets of the United States. Since most spearing has been banned, except for Aboriginal people in the United States, much of the dive fishing has fallen by the wayside. It has often been viewed as unethical by some people. It is, nevertheless, a fishing technique once used by many fishers, even in North America.

Greedy little minds are ever busy turning landscapes into slag heaps, housing tracts, canals, freeways and shopping malls, a perversion they zealously pursue under the ragged banner of progress.

–Sheridan Anderson, *The Curtis Creek Manifesto*

Putting Fido to Work

One technique, which can only be described as totally obscure, is the little known art of fishing with dogs. The domestic dog is known as our "best friend" and has been trained by humans for a multitude of tasks. In various parts of the world, dogs have even been taught to help catch fish. In Tierra del Fuego, for example, the ancient inhabitants trained their dogs to drive fish into their nets by corralling the fish in one area toward nets and scaring the fish into the enclosed mesh, where the nets can then be lifted and the fish removed from the water. In Asia, an ancient Aboriginal tribe in Northern Japan had actually trained the domestic dog to swim in the water in packs, much like wolves, and corral fish into shallow water where they could be captured and pulled out. It is said that the Aboriginals would reward their specially trained fishing dogs with fish heads, a way of enticing them into pack fishing. Dogs have also been reported to be able to capture crabs with their claws and to remain fishing on their own without human supervision. So the old saying, you can't teach an old dog new tricks, I suppose, may not necessarily be true when it comes to fishing.

Shocking Fishing Experience

Electroshocking is a technique used most often by fishery biologists as a way of collecting and housing specimens temporarily to be processed as a sample in a fishery study. In my days at Sir Sanford Fleming College School of Natural Resources in Lindsay, Ontario, we carried out several electroshock projects on trout streams. There are also ongoing electroshock studies of the Lake Ontario fishery carried out by the Metro Toronto and Region Conservation Authority.

Electro shocking is a method in which electric probes are sent into the water column, sending out an electric current that temporarily stuns the fish and pulls them towards the probes. Researchers can then net the fish easily and transfer them to live wells. Electroshock fishing carried out on smaller streams is done with a special "electro backpack" that sends out a much weaker signal and is used for sampling smaller fish species such as minnow, ground fish or smaller members of the trout family. Electroshocking is particularly effective in that it leaves no permanent damage on the fish and allows for easy access to specimens for ongoing fishery management studies. I can recall, from the work I did with Metro Toronto and Region Conservation Authority, that different fish species react differently to the shocking probes. Heartier fish like the brown trout, salmon and rainbow trout were quick to revive following the experience, while ground fish such as the common carp and white fish were much slower to recover. Electroshocking is a technique that very few people will ever see, but once you have, you will never forget seeing the fish pulled toward the boat as if by a vacuum.

> *I don't want to catch a fish, I felt like*
> *shouting. I can't. I am a prisoner hemmed*
> *in by walls of trees and branches. The long*
> *rod does not want to work in these conditions.*
> *I am hot and I look absurd.*

–Margot Page, *Little Rivers*

Flipping

Flipping is a fishing technique most commonly used to catch largemouth and smallmouth bass. It is actually a casting technique carried out in a smooth, underhand motion and often employed close to shore or in and around the structure where fish hang out. Professional bass anglers use flipping with great success during tournaments when there is heavy pressure and boat traffic on the water. The advantage of flipping is that it is a great way to offer a gentle presentation with minimal disruption in the water. A properly flipped lure presented with pinpoint accuracy will often enter the water with barely a sound.

The flipper will gauge the amount of line he needs in order to launch his bait in a pendulum-like action so as to drop it in right next to fish holding tight to cover. Although it is a productive way to fish under certain conditions, proper tackle is also required. Equipment tackle manufacturers now produce rod and reel combinations specifically made for flipping. It is without a doubt the most finesse-based fishing technique out there used by many of the better sport anglers today.

Poisoning

Fish poisoning, although technically a fish-catching technique, has been received with great controversy over the years. Some cultures still use poisoning through extracts from ichthyotoxic plants. They crush the plant and sprinkle the poison in the water, causing the fish in the nearby area to float to the surface in search of air, making their capture easy. Since the poison in these plants is fairly mild and dilutes easily in water, it must be carried out in a small area, otherwise it would not be effective. Some Aboriginals of the Xingu Tribe in Brazil will even bait their fish hooks with the ichthyotoxic plant extract and as soon as a fish strikes, of course, the toxins go to work rendering it helpless and it rises to the surface.

Another form of fish poisoning in history is the use of lime. Common lime used in landscaping or as a fertilizing additive has also been used to poison fish, but perhaps the most common chemical poison used to catch fish is rotenone. Fishing with the rotenone at the right dosage is almost always lethal. Again, under the supervision of a trained biologist, rotenone is administered to completely kill off all fish in the area with the idea of lake reclamation. Lake reclamation is the complete destruction of all living fish within a water body, without contaminating the water. After an application or two of rotenone and all unwanted fish species have been eradicated, aquaculture and hatching/stocking will usually take place, and the water body will be replenished with a more viable species.

…angling-rod and reel, troutline, jugline, grabbling, whatever—offers possibly our last link with the eternal verities of nature and pursuit. And no better fish to pursue than the one with whiskers.

–M.H. Dutch Salmon, *The Catfish as Metaphor*

Bow Fishing

With the increase in popularity of bow hunting in North America for game animals, the idea of bow fishing was born. People who fish with bows use similar equipment to any archer, whether a bow hunter or target shooter. A compound bow with aluminum or carbon arrows is the most popular equipment for bow fishing. It is a sport carried out in many parts of central and southern United States and is said to be very difficult given the accuracy required for a successful hit. Target species for bow fishers are usually large, less desirable fish, such as the carp or white sucker. Bow fishing requires a special attachment on the arrow which allows for better contact with the fish, and each arrow on a bow outfit must also be equipped with a retrieval line. Bow fishing is really just one more morph of the spear or dive fishing but is nonetheless a bona fide sport and one more of the many fishing techniques found in North America.

Chapter Eight

Facts on Youth Fishing Today

Although we have witnessed a trend in recent days toward a reliance on natural resources and an overall increase in fishing participation, there is one area still lagging behind: the participation of young people in sportfishing today. According to a report by the National Sporting Goods Association, there has been a noticeable decline in youth involvement in outdoor activities such as biking, swimming and fishing. Young people aged seven to 17 are simply not going fishing as much as they used to. Angling participation in the United States fell 10.4 percent between 1994 and 2004.

This decline in youth fishing sends out a clear message of the shifting interests of today's society. But it doesn't need to be that way, and we owe it to ourselves to buck this trend and head back out on the water. Fishing, in my opinion, is every bit as exciting as the best video game system on the market. Adrenaline junkies of the modern age are into the fast and furious with constant action and stimulation. The same experience can easily be had with a fishing rod and some bait. Enticing a fish into striking requires patience, self-control and commitment—attributes that also make a good video gamer—and that moment when it all comes together is cash-in time. An angler's senses must be acute and reflexes at the ready. Fighting a fish—on many levels—is like a good video game and the best part is that it's real life. In the ongoing battle of man against nature, the outcome truly is in our hands, and if you ask me, reality is way cooler than virtual reality!

But if sheer excitement isn't enough, Canada and the United States also have incentive programs and activities to entice young people away from the X-Box and towards the tackle box.

National Fishing Week in Canada

National Fishing Week (NFW) is Canada's largest promotion of community-based sport-fishing and conservation activities for youth today. The idea of NFW is to put aside a full week in July dedicated to the preservation of the sport and to encourage kids to participate in fishing in one way or another with a range of activities across the country. NFW achieves this by gearing their activities towards the interests of young people today by establishing hands-on training sessions and often providing free fishing equipment to those who participate. We are getting people involved. Fishing derbies held during NFW are extremely popular because of the prizes, participation and involvement of young people. It is a time to celebrate the sport and get involved in fishing. It is events like NFW that will help solidify the future of fishing.

Kids All-American Fishing Derby

The Kids All-American Fishing Derby is an event in the United States, similar to National Fishing Week in Canada, where families and children are encouraged to get involved in a series of fishing events. At present, there are more than 2000 local events set up in all 50 states promoting fishing with kids, and at last count, over 400,000 children of all ages took part in various derbies and events across the United States. The idea of the Kids All-American Fishing Derby actually began in 1986, spawned from a suggestion by the Fishing Tackle Industry Association, as an idea of stimulating kids' interest in the sport. At the time, the executive director of Hooked on Fishing International (HOFI) ran with the idea and developed the concept of a fishing derby where local communities could get involved and non-anglers would be exposed to sportfishing in their community. They provided kits that included rods and reels, bobbers, souvenir decals, award certificates and so on. Since 2000, the event has incorporated the Fuji Film Fish Photograph and Release program with the idea of teaching kids about catch and release and other ethical practices around the sport. As an added incentive, any child who enters their photograph and a short essay about conservation has the chance to win a $1000 savings bond.

The true fisherman approaches the first day of fishing with all the sense of wonder and awe of a child approaching Christmas.

–Robert Traver, *Trout Madness*

Youth Fishing Academy

Even fishing charters such as the Inshore Slam Fishing Charters of Tampa, Florida, understand the importance of youth fishing. This program of fishing seminars as part of a youth fishing academy is something new in the United States, but it seems to be catching on. The academy is a fishing school designed to expose kids to fishing and the experiences that will broaden their understanding in three key areas: fishing, boating and environmental conservation. Captain Savaglio runs a program along with several of his captains, covering topics like equipment, bait, lure selection, rod building techniques, rigging, casting instructions, casting skills tournament strategies, fish fighting skills, handling, environmental and conservation issues and catch and release. The Youth Fishing Academy runs different formats over the course of several days on the water in the Tampa area.

American Youth Fishing Association

The American Youth Fishing Association (AYFA) is a non-profit organization based out of Southern California. The AYFA is run by a team of avid fishermen with the idea of sharing the enthusiasm and benefits of sportfishing with young people. Their mission statement is "the dedication to the preservation of ocean and freshwater fisheries."

They represent fishermen from the United States, Canada and Central and South America who look to pass on the love of the sport as a legacy to future generations. The youth fishing programs sponsored by the AYFA are established with the hopes of introducing the youth to the appreciation of nature and the beauty and bounty of American oceans, lakes, rivers and streams. The AYFA has a series of organized events throughout the year in different communities as well as a wide range of sponsors and organized conservation events. Through the AYFA, thousands of kids are getting an opportunity to catch their first fish, take their very first boat ride and experience the beautiful Pacific Ocean off the coast of California.

Did you know?

A starfish doesn't have a brain and can have up to 16 arms!

Ontario Family Fishing Weekend

The province of Ontario is doing its part to encourage fishing among its young people today. It now has two family fishing weekends established—one during the wintertime in February and another one in July. The idea of Family Fishing Weekend is to make it easier for young people to get exposed to the sport. For these two special weekends each year, the government waives the fishing license requirement as a way to make it easier for young people to participate without having to shell out any cash. Of course, all anglers must still abide by conservation license limits set out in the Ontario Recreational Fishing Regulation Summary.

Youth of Atlantic Canada

The Newfoundland & Labrador Minister of Tourism, Culture and Recreation hit the nail on the head with regards to youth fishing in Canada. In an initiative they call Youth Hunting and Fishing Exchange Program, residents of Prince Edward Island, New Brunswick, Nova Scotia and Newfoundland & Labrador between the ages of 12 to 17 are eligible to participate in an outdoor-related exchange contest. Entry forms for the program are included in each province's fishing guidelines book and include the opportunity to travel to one of Atlantic Canada's other provinces to enjoy a fishing adventure.

Thanks to combined efforts from Atlantic Canada's various ministry departments, kids are given the chance to go on a trip like Curtis Glover of Trinity, Newfoundland, did when he won an all-expenses paid trip to Prince Edward Island. According to the Minister, the program provides

an opportunity for young people throughout the region to experience the diverse culture that is found in the Atlantic Provinces.

For inexperienced anglers, a day of fishing has the potential to be either the most exciting or the most monotonous time of their life. It may sound like a cliché, but sport fishing really is what you make of it and getting started on the right foot is key to making it work.

–Jeff Morrison, "A Primer for the First Timer," *Toronto SUN*

Trailblazer Adventure Program

Early in 2009, the B.A.S.S. organization and its youth division teamed up with the United States Sportsman's Alliance to formalize a relationship with the Trailblazer Adventure Program and to provide further outdoor education including fishing at the Boy Scouts of America camps nationwide. The B.A.S.S. members set up education stations at the various camps, and lessons included elements of "Casting Kids" with a focus on techniques of baiting, lure selection, fish regulations, boating safety and conservation.

Budd Pigeon of the Trailblazer Adventure Program said they are looking to increase the reach of their program and working with organizations like B.A.S.S. was a natural fit to give a positive spin to fishing as a recreational activity. The Trailblazer Adventure Program is the largest outdoor program of its kind and has fostered the interest in outdoor activities such as fishing to more than 700,000 youths and families since 2001. In the year 2008 alone, the Trailblazer Adventure Program held 75 events in 34 states across the country, for a total of one 179,000 participants.

A trout river is like a book: some parts are dull and some are lively.

–H.G. Tapply, *The Sportsman's Notebook*

Fish for the Future

Rodney Hsu of British Columbia's beautiful Fraser Valley has dedicated his life to sportfishing and maintains a website based out of Steveston that caters to a wide range of different levels of anglers. Rod's "Fish for the Future" program is an event he holds each year in honor of our angling youth. It is a one-day community festival that takes place during the National Fishing Week in Canada with the goal of promoting sportfishing and other outdoor activities to kids

and families in British Columbia. Throughout the day, participants can get involved in such activities as fly casting, fly tying, fish and insect identification as well as fun games to keep the kids involved.

The Learn to Fish Program

The Freshwater Fisheries Society of British Columbia is another organization funded in part from the sale of fishing licenses and is responsible for various trout-stocking programs across the province. The Learn to Fish program is an initiative geared towards introducing new participants to the sport. It is the perfect fit for youth and families of British Columbia and has been a tremendous success thus far, reaching over 30,000 young people and their families across the province. Some of the topics covered are habitat and conservation; proper fish handling and ethics; safety and fishing regulations and where, when and how to catch fish. It is a comprehensive and hands-on program and is being met with very positive reviews.

An old phrase evokes the fly-fisherman's
spring: the sweet of the year.

–R. Palmer Baker, *The Sweet of the Year*

Chapter Nine

Modern-day Fish & Fishing: Odds & Sods

In North America today, sport and commercial fishing play a more pivotal role in society and the world's economy than ever before. Various interest groups, organizations, clubs and associations are now established to manage and oversee the various facets of fishing. There is a laundry list of fishing conservation groups that practice habitat management, and there are many more local fishing clubs than ever before. Fishing and fish today are not only important as a renewable natural resource, but they are also big money. As we work our way through a global recession, a return to the basics of life in the form of fishing seems to be the way of the future. Why not conserve now what we have for our children's children to enjoy and benefit from?

Fish are important on so many levels it's mind-boggling. The fragility of fish stocks on a global scale has forced world organizations to put serious thought into preserving these populations. The money and enjoyment gained by the many interest groups and factions that dedicate themselves to the conservation of various fish species should not be understated.

On top of high-profile fisheries conservation activities, some of the strangest fishing-related behavior is going on these days. Anglers are resorting to some odd tactics to catch and even consume fish, from highfalutin fishing tackle to fishing tools so strange they must certainly have been dreamed up by Maxwell Smart himself. We will see in this chapter how fish are not only big business in modern-day North America, but also how they have taken on a life of their own as the subject of strange fascination.

Weird Facts about Sushi

The practice of eating sushi has become so popular today that sushi bars and sushi chefs can be found at almost every street corner. Eating sushi has become a rite of passage for not only older working-class people but for young people and families as well. Sushi can be purchased at the grocery store, in restaurants or online; it can be served fresh, frozen or anywhere in between. There are some facts about sushi, however, that few people may even realize and most of which will surprise you. In Japan, sushi chefs in their apprenticeship must spend a minimum of two years learning how to cook and season rice, plus another three years in training to properly prepare the fish before being allowed to work behind a sushi bar. In North America, however, there is such a high demand for the product and sushi chefs that they may work behind the bar after only a few months of basic training.

It is also a little known fact too that today's sushi actually began as a type of fast food, and was the 19th century Japanese equivalent to McDonald's.

A sushi chef's knives are actually miniature versions of samurai swords with blades that must be sharpened and re-sharpened daily.

Sushi today that is served fresh is often less fresh than the frozen sushi available.

One of the most popular types of fish used to make sushi, the yellowtail, is actually factory farmed now and is similar to veal in that they are fattened until their muscles disintegrate while they are still alive.

Many people believe that sushi, as well as many fish species, is extremely healthy and good for you. The truth of the matter is that most sushi rolls served in North America are loaded with salt and heavy in fats and carbohydrates.

It is also a little known fact that the most expensive ingredient of today's sushi, the belly meat of the bluefin tuna, was actually once despised by the Japanese—so much so that they once considered it unfit for human consumption.

Very few people realize that the mass production we see today of sushi rolls was actually pioneered by a female scientist in Britain back in the 1940s. In fact, there is actually a shrine in her memory located in Japan.

Despite all the myths and mysteries of sushi, it is one fish product that is bursting with popularity across North America.

A Virtual Fishing Fantasy

In December 2007, FLW Fantasy Fishing was created and took flight. With the advent of modern technology and the increasing reliance on virtual reality and a trend away from industriousness, the idea of fantasy fishing was born. What better way for the armchair fisher of modern day to feel the excitement of being on the water and to have the opportunity to win large amounts of money? Each participant in fantasy fishing picks one of 10 real-life professional anglers, along with how they feel that angler will finish in any number of given tournaments. It is similar to fantasy football or picking horses at the track, although in this case it is a group of professional anglers out on the water and their ability to catch a lot of fish.

The FLW Fantasy Fishing participants earn points based on their team and are awarded prizes throughout the fishing season, which run anywhere from $100,000 to more than $1 million depending on the event. The Professional Fishing Tour, which features many different bass, walleye and other pro fishing events throughout North America, is closely tied in to the FLW Fantasy Fishing. The big difference is that fantasy fishing participants are not actually fishing. They are sitting in the comfort of their home and living vicariously through the professional anglers they can watch live on television. It is this type of event that appeals to modern-day young people who get their kicks from reality-based, super adrenaline infused pastimes of today. FLW Fantasy Fishing captures the excitement of real fishing and includes huge cash payouts. It is what I would call modern fishing excitement for those who are not necessarily able to make it out on the water.

Did you know?

The lungfish can live out of water for as long as four years!

The North American Fishing Club

The North American Fishing Club is an organization that typifies the modern angler. It is now the largest fishing club in the world and you'll see there is little wonder why it has become successful. Since fishing has always been considered a team activity and a bonding pastime, a North American-wide fishing club is the perfect idea for getting people together. Because of its huge buying and bargaining power, club members have the ability to gain access to the latest and greatest products on the market today. This is a benefit that was usually only enjoyed by outdoor writers and other fishing professionals who provided ongoing exposure for tackle manufacturers and therefore gained access to free fishing equipment.

Anglers join organizations like the North American Fishing Club these days for the camaraderie, and for the deals and discounts offered through the club. There are also features like the Fishing Resource Directory, which includes a complete rundown of the top guides and charter services in Canada and the U.S. Members can also gain access to events in their community and in other areas and can participate as correspondents in the club. Members regularly submit fishing reports online—a benefit to other members and a great way to keep in touch with what is going on in the world of fishing. The North American Fishing Club is just one more example of the way fishing is headed today. It may seem high profile and a way of glorifying the sport, yet it is of great benefit to the resource by promoting catch and release and other various conservation initiatives.

World's Smallest Fishing Boat

Call me a big kid at heart, but anything remote controlled is okay in my books. So when I heard about a new remote-controlled fishing boat, I got a warm and fuzzy feeling inside. The Fishin' Buddy by Aviva is honestly one of the neatest angling tools I have ever seen, and although I believe it to be a gadget more geared towards youth anglers, many

people today will get a kick out of it. The Fishin'
Buddy is a unique remote-controlled boat that
actually catches fish. With two deeply inset propel-
lers, swivel fishing line attachment and a gaff for
retrieving the boat when a fish is on, the Fishin'
Buddy is basically a fishing rod and reel all rolled
into one. Once you maneuver the boat into position
and your line sinks, be ready with the controls to
give 'er some gas! When a fish strikes you simply
press the hand control and steer your boat—and
fish—back into shore. My girls and I caught several good-sized fish before the battery needed
recharging, and we had a hoot in the process.

Fish Food with a Kick!

Another weird fact about fish and fishing in
society today is the number of strange fish dishes
used as table fare across North America. One such
odd fish meal is fugu, a fish eaten as a delicacy in
Japan and other parts of Asia. The fugu is a blowfish with extremely deadly poison within its
organs, yet many around the world eat it as an
expensive meal. In Japan, there is an expression
that goes, "I want to eat fugu but I don't want to
die." This expression has come about as the result
of some instantaneous deaths from restaurant-
goers who have eaten improperly prepared fugu.
In Japan, only very skilled and licensed chefs are
even allowed to prepare fugu for their clients as

there are strict regulations now in place on the use of this deadly blowfish as table fare.

Not only is this dangerous fish meal high profile because of its deadly after effects, the cost per serving is outrageously high. It may cost as much as $200 or more per person and sometimes more, depending on the chef. According to people in the blowfish community, the most poisonous fugu of all, known as torafugu, is also the most delicious and the most expensive of the fugu dishes. This deadly dish, as I discovered, is actually now sold online and in some grocery stores in Japan. Winter is evidently the best season to eat this fish as there seems to be less risk of dying at this time. I think I will stick to trout and walleye, thank-you very much.

*An undisturbed river is as perfect as we will
ever know, every refractive slide of cold water a
glimpse of eternity.*

–Thomas McGuane, *Midstream, an Outside Chance*

Main Stream Table Fare

Best Health magazine is a publication that promotes fine cuisine, fitness and various aspects of healthy eating today. In an article they featured on fish as a meal, they rated the top six fish to eat based on health benefits and nutritional value. In the number six position as the healthiest fish to eat are sardines, herring and anchovies out of the can. According to the experts, these three fish are loaded with omega-3s, which help prevent many diseases including cancer, heart disease and arthritis, and they help increase brain function and overall immunity. They are very low in contaminates and are extremely eco-friendly. Some people find the fish have a strong flavor; however, chefs have discovered various ways to limit the strong taste.

Number five in the best fish to eat category is the sablefish, otherwise known as black cod. It is a white, mild fish with very flaky fillets and a rich flavor. Chefs often call this a butter fish because of its buttery texture. According to the experts, it is also a great source of omega-3s. Sablefish is also a great source of selenium. According to registered dietitian Mary Sue Waisman, selenium is a trace mineral that may help protect cells from damage. Sablefish are found mostly in the North Pacific, and their populations are stable.

Number four on the list according to this magazine is the Atlantic mackerel. The Atlantic mackerel is often marketed as "Round" when sold as a fresh, uncleaned fish. It is a great table fish with a full-bodied flavor. Some people find mackerel too strong, but its benefits override its powerful taste. According to the experts, mackerel is loaded with omega-3s. It also contains a lot of vitamin B12, which is another important vitamin in today's diet because it helps every single cell in our bodies work properly. The contamination of heavy metals and chemicals is an important fact of eating fish today, and this risk is low in mackerel according to experts.

Number three on the best fish list is the Pacific halibut. The Pacific halibut is a firm white meat with a mild flavor that appeals to many non-fish eaters because of its mild, flavorful taste. Halibut actually contains an entire day's worth of omega-3s. According to experts, it is also extremely low in fat and is a great source of potassium and vitamin D.

As far as eco-friendliness goes, the Pacific halibut has been given the green light by American conservation groups.

Number two on the list is rainbow trout. Its delicate flesh has a nutty flavor similar to salmon, only milder. One serving of rainbow trout has more than one day's intake of omega-3s, as well as a lot of vitamin B12. Most rainbow trout found in Canadian stores are hatchery trout, and because they rarely escape into natural waters, there is little risk of contamination from mercury or other metals. Trout are a popular fish in today's society and, thanks to aquaculture, are readily available for the dinner table.

And the number one best fish to eat, according to *Best Health*, is wild Pacific salmon, which includes fresh and canned Chinook, king, chum, Coho, pink and sockeye salmon. Salmon are a versatile fish with a pleasant and distinctive aroma and meaty flesh. Every salmon is extremely high in omega-3s. Salmon is also a good source of vitamin B, and canned salmon, since the bones are canned as well, may be a good source of calcium.

There you have the top five best fish for eating and trust me, the popularity of fish as table fare in today's society is overwhelming. Fish are and have always been considered brain food and perhaps the healthiest source of protein.

Tackle for the More Affluent

The average fishing lure in North America would cost on average, I would say, $5 or so. But what if I told you there were manufacturers out there that charge hundreds, thousands and even $1 million per lure? It is the brainchild of MacDaddy's Fishing Lures to create this outrageous line of gifts in keeping with the passion of fishing and the excitement of having a fish on the end of your line. At MacDaddy's, they believe in living life to the fullest.

Can you imagine that same excitement of catching a fish with not your run-of-the-mill crank bait, but a diamond encrusted, solid gold fishing lure? With over 40 years of combined experience in marketing these priceless lures, and with product lines currently available ranging from $40,000 to $1 million, those at MacDaddy's say there is a little something for everyone. Perhaps it is a gimmick or the latest craze in status symbols for the angling rich, but these finely crafted lures and flies are works of art from what I have seen.

McDaddy's features items from spoons of solid gold and many diamonds to jeweled flies in a variety of gemstones including diamonds, rubies and sapphires. They are nothing short of works of art, but what anglers would want to fish with a $9000 fly on the end of a line? It is another one of those unexplained gimmicks and oddities found in an already strange sport.

And, if a $9000 fishing fly isn't your bag and you have really got something to prove, try out MacDaddy's flagship lure called the Million Dollar Lure. "Make a bold statement," says MacDaddy, by using this glimmering three pounds of gold and platinum encrusted with diamonds and rubies, containing a staggering 4753 gemstones. It is nearly 12 inches in length and is billed as a big game lure. The Million Dollar Lure created quite a fuss recently in a tournament in Cabo San Lucas when the press took turns photographing a wealthy angler who was casting this million-dollar gem. If that is out of your price

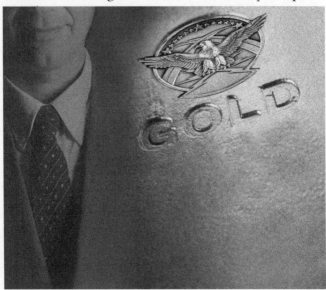

range, MacDaddy's does have products as cheap as $500 to $700 for a 14-carat solid gold fishing fly with 38 diamonds. I would imagine that for anyone who can afford this luxurious tackle, the idea of losing one of these fishing gems to the bite of a large fish is probably of little concern.

*...when a lawyer is swallowed up with busi-
ness and the statesman is preventing or con-
triving plots, then we sit on cowslip-banks,
hear the birds sing, and possess ourselves in as
much quietness as these silent silver streams.*

–Izaak Walton, *The Compleat Angler*

Fishing and Night Vision

Since anglers of today, myself included, have discovered that fishing after dark has its advantages, many have resorted to heading out on the water only after the sun goes down. With the fishing pressure increasing on many lakes and rivers, the commotion and boat traffic often spook the fish to the point that they become active only after the dust has settled. Although not used extensively as a fishing aid, Bushnell Night Vision products have their place among the sportfishing enthuiasts of today. Whether it is the digital color monocular, the goggles or the binoculars, all these products, believe it or not, have their purpose and use within the small but growing nighttime fishing community.

As strange as it may sound to most, many anglers find that use of these "starlight scopes" creates safer boating and improved visibility when traveling to and from your favorite fishing hot spot. Bushnell, the world's leader in optics, makes a Digital Color Night Vision monocular, which can be used when traveling on the water to identify lake structure and obstacles while fishing. The company's Night Vision headset comes in handy when taking care of tasks in the boat, such as handling fish, changing lures and maneuvering your craft around tight spaces on the water. I even have a pair of Bushnell Night Vision binoculars that I use regularly while on the water to identify structures and as a safety precaution while traveling from spot to spot. This technology was once believed to be a gadget used only by the military, but not anymore. Not only does night vision allow anglers to travel more safely after dark, but it makes most tasks in the boat easier after the sun goes down.

World's Most Dangerous Fish

Another strange fact of fish today is the danger that they pose to us as far as consumption and sharing our environment. Certain fish species are downright dangerous. Take the Portuguese man o'war for example. Although it resembles a jellyfish, the man o'war is actually a collection of sea animals carried by the current of the Gulf Stream. Man o' wars are found as far south as Australia and may measure as small as six inches across, but they possess tentacles that can reach 40 feet in length. These tentacles can inflict a nasty sting; however, the sting is rarely fatal.

Cone shells are another dangerous feature of the oceans today. Cone shells have tiny teeth similar to hypodermic needles, and if stepped on, will inject extremely dangerous venom, causing acute pain, paralysis and potential death within a few short hours.

The weaver fish is another ocean fish to be avoided. They are tropical, about 12 inches long and slim in configuration and contain venomous spines all over their body that can inflict a painful wound.

The toadfish, which also dwells in tropical waters off the coast of South America, is another critter to stay away from. The toadfish buries itself in the sand and can be easily stepped on by divers and swimmers alike. The toadfish has extremely poisonous spines on its dorsal fin.

The surgeonfish is a deep bodied, small mouthed, bright-looking tropical fish with needle-like spines on the back of its tail. The surgeonfish is found throughout the tropics and can inflict some painful wounds on anyone who gets swiped by its tail.

The stonefish is one of the most dangerous little fish in the South Pacific and Indian Oceans. Although it is only about 12 inches long and its drab coloring makes it look fairly innocuous, the fins eject an extremely powerful poison that is also extremely painful and can be fatal.

The scorpion fish is another species of the Pacific and Indian Oceans. They are usually reddish in color and possess long wavy fins. They, too, can inflict a painful sting.

The rabbit fish, another dangerous species of the Pacific and Indian Oceans, possesses long, venomous and sharp spines that are quite painful if stepped on.

Stingrays, as we have heard, also have the potential to be dangerous. They have a distinct ray shape, but their colors may vary. The venomous barbed spines near the tail can cause severe or fatal injury if they penetrate the skin.

Other dangerous saltwater fish include the barracuda, which has been known to take nasty bites out of swimmers and divers, as well as the

morey eel and the sea bass. Morey eels are extremely aggressive if disturbed, and sea bass are dangerous because of their sheer size, as they grow quite huge. Sea bass have been known to bite off large pieces of flesh from humans who get too close.

One of the few dangerous freshwater fish is the piranha. This famous little creature with a giant bite is an inhabitant of the tropics and northern regions of South America. Piranhas are usually quite small but possess extremely large teeth and travel in large schools. It is said that a school of piranhas can devour a 230-pound hog in a matter of minutes.

Other potential dangers in freshwater are the pike and muskellunge. Muskie have been known to attack swimmers or dangling legs that look like a wounded minnow. Attacks, however, by pike and muskie are extremely rare.

To me, bream on a fly rod are as pretty fishing as a man can want, but there are times when they aren't worth working for.

–John Graves, *Goodbye to a River*

Sportfishing in America Today

The economic impact of sportfishing in the United States is staggering. It is said that the over 40 million sports anglers in the United States generate a whopping $45 billion dollars in retail sales each year. According to the latest Fish and Wildlife Service Report, the sportfishing industry also creates a $125-billion impact on the nation's overall economy and provides employment for more than one million people, so its impact on today's society is an important fact of fishing today. According to statistics in the United States, there are more Americans who fish regularly than play golf or tennis combined, and there are an estimated 24.4 million golfers in the U.S. and 10.4 million avid tennis players. With 40 million sports fishermen and women, that is 33 times the average attendance per game at all major league baseball clubs combined.

The National Sporting Goods Association ranked fishing sixth out of 42 recreational activities, preceded only by walking, swimming, exercising, camping and bowling. The benefits to the U.S. economy also have a trickle-down effect in the area of conservation, as a portion of license sales goes towards conservation of fish species, and in 2006, license sales alone topped out at over $600 million. The amount of federal tax generated by anglers' spending in one year alone was over $9 billion, or roughly equal to the entire 2006 budget for the U.S. Environmental Protection Agency.

Great Underwater View

Jeff Zernov was one of the founding members of *In Fisherman* magazine along with Al Lindner and Ron Lindner. Zernov and the Lindners had the idea back in the late 1970s of observing objects below the surface through the fish's eyes. They even put forward a scientific formula that included a fish-eye view of underwater life. Zernov left *In Fisherman* in the 1980s and started an electronics company called Zircom Corporation, which manufactured sonars and marine electronics. As time went on, the new company, now known as Nature Vision, became the authority on the angler's underwater eye. Their product, Aquaview, is now being used by over 150,000 anglers across North America.

The Aquaview Underwater Viewing System is like a small monitor attached to your fishing lure at all times. The Aquaview comes with a screen monitoring device that allows you to keep tabs on what is going on under the surface. Inquiring minds of today's modern angler love nothing more than keeping on top of the latest technology, and Aquaview is one of the specialized gadgets that most anglers only dream of having at their disposal. There are various applications for Aquaview, but all basically provide the same end result: a real-time underwater look at what is going on near your lure or bait. It is one of those fishing gadgets that's almost too good to be true.

When you are next complaining about the selectivity of trout, bear the thought in mind: were it not for this fortunate trait, how long would our stream fishing last?

–Art Flick, *Art Flick's Streamside Guide*

Radio Controlled Feed Boat

Much the same concept as the Aviva Fishin' Buddy, the Radio Controlled Feed Boat is a remote controlled boat that will bring your bait and floats to distances unreachable by a conventional cast, up to 985 feet from your location. The Feed Boat has built-in sonar, a tipper with a capacity of 4.4 pounds of bait and an underwater LED light with a range of up to 948 feet. The display on the remote control shows you where to find the fish and at which depth the shovel is moving. It also shows water temperature and will dispense bait at the touch of a button. It will also dispense your baited hook if you like. The Feed Boat is powered by two jet motors located in the hull that allow you to navigate quietly through algae and waters with a lot of structure. With a retail price of just slightly over $800, it is not a gadget that many anglers today can readily afford.

Making Fish Leather

Making leather from fish skins is one of those activities I consider to be a fringe activity, as very few people would ever consider it. However, in keeping with the complete and full use of a fish after harvesting, it seems like a great idea. According to experts, it is also quite easy to make fish leather. First, gather various fish skins from any fish that you have filleted, or else any fish market that prepares fish fillets for sale may be able to provide the skins at no charge. Scrape off excess flesh using a fleshing knife and soak them in a saline solution for several days. After soaking, completely scale the skins, which may take some time. Professional leather manufacturers actually have a special chemical that will help release the scales. Short of that, scales must be hand-picked and scraped off completely.

Then thoroughly detox the skin, which basically means it should be washed well to remove any natural oils or chemicals. Soak the clean skins in pickling brine for up to two years, a process that preserves the skins without requiring refrigeration.

Now the tricky part: get the bark from the Australian gum tree to create an organic non-toxic tanning solution. Press the bark into every pore of the skin to ensure that there is proper cover throughout. After covering the fish skin with the tanning solution, the leather may be dried between two sheets of absorbent cloth, similar to the technique for pressing a flower. Your near-complete fish leather may be waterproofed by pouring a glaze, a wax or a resin over it and thoroughly drying it. The final product is a fine, very supple leather, similar to eel skin, which can be used for a variety of purposes. There is considerable time involved in making fish leather, but those interested in using every part of the fish they harvest may also be interested in a different, more exotic use for the fish body parts.

I continually read of men who said they could be just as happy not catching trout as catching them. To me, that even then sounded pious nonsense, and rather more of an excuse than a statement of fact…No, I want to get them, and every time I slip on a wader, and put up a fly, it is this in mind.

–Brian Clarke, *The Pursuit of the Stillwater Trout*

Notes on Sources

American Sportfishing Association. *US Fish & Wildlife Service Report*. Washington: Smithsonian Institution Press, 2006.

American Sportfishing Association. *Sportfishing in America*. Washington: Smithsonian Institution Press, 2008.

Brandt, Von. *Fish Catching Methods of the World—4th Edition*. Oxford, UK: Blackwell Publishing, 2005.

"Shipwrecked". *Deadliest Catch*. Discovery Channel, 2009.

Fisheries Research & Development Corporation. *Vol 16, Number 4. Fishing Dangers*. Sydney: Australian Government Press, 2008.

Fisheries and Oceans Canada. *Canadian Science Advisory Secretariat—Asian Carp Status Report*. Ottawa: Government of Canada. 2005

Lyons, Nick. *The Quotable Fisherman*. New York: Mainstreet Publishing Company, 1998.

Morey, Shaun. *Incredible Fishing Stories: Vol 1*. New York: Workman Publishing, 1993.

Waldman, John. *100 Weird Ways to Catch Fish*. New York: Stockpole Books, 2005.

Web Sources

America Sportfishing Association: Sportfishing in America. CSIA. http://www.asafishing.org (accessed July 20 to August 12, 2009)

Antique Lure Collecting Articles by Dr. Michael Echols. http://www.antiquelures.com/ (accessed July 20 to August 22, 2009)

"Aqua-Vu Story." Aquavu. http://www.aquavu.com/learn-more/articles/article.html/43 (accessed October 20-22, 2009)

"Banning Micklow & Bull LLP Sport Fishing, Charter and Ferry Claims." http://www.maritimetriallawyers.com/ (accessed July 20-22, 2009)

"The Best Fish to Eat." Best Health Magazine: Health and Fitness. CSIA. http://www.besthealthmag.ca (accessed October 20-21, 2009)

Blackfeather Charters—Prince Rupert BC: http://www.blackfeathercharters.com/ (accessed September 20-22, 2009)

Canadian Sportfishing Industry Association: Industry news and Issues. CSIA. Canadian Sportfishing Industry Association http://www.csia.ca/media/media.htm (accessed July 20 to August 1, 2009)

Canadian Sportfishing Industry Association: Industry News and Issues. CSIA. Canadian Sportfishing Industry Association http://www.csia.ca/media/media.htm (accessed July 20 to August 1, 2009)

Coolest –Gadgets.com Radio-Controlled Feed Boat. http://www.coolest-gadgets.com/20090804/radiocontrolled-feed-boat/ (accessed October 20 to November 20, 2009)

"Cheetah Power Surge." D'Angelo Brands. http://www.dangelobrands.ca/index.shtml (accessed October 20 to November 20, 2009)

eHow—How to Make Fish Leather. http://www.ehow.com/ (accessed October 20 to November 1, 2009)

"Fishing with Rod." Fish for the Future 2009: http://www.fishingwithrod.com (accessed September 20-25, 2009)

Fish Online: Angling Methods. CSIA. http://www.fishonline.org/information/methods (accessed October 20-25, 2009)

Florida Sportfishing. The Zone. http://floridasportfishing.com/magazine/safe-boating/the-zone-3.html (accessed July 1-25, 2009)

"Learn to Fish." Freshwater Fisheries Society of BC. http://www.gofishbc.com/ (accessed November 1-20, 2009)

Government of Newfoundland & Labrador. Tourism, Culture and Recreation -News Releases. http://www.newsreleases.com/ (accessed July 20-22, 2009)

Governor's Advisory Council for Hunting, Fishing & Conservation. Hunting & Fishing Participation Among the Nation's Youth: http://www.dcnr.state.pa.us/gsac/participation.aspx (accessed September 20 to October 22, 2009)

MacDaddy's Fishing Lures Inc. http://www.macdaddysfishinglures.com/ (accessed October 20 to November 01, 2009)

Mike Bolton Casting Blind. ESPN Outdoors Fishing http://espn.go.com/outdoors (accessed July 1 to October 30, 2009)

Mr. Lure Box—Antique Fishing Lures: http://www.mrlurebox.com/ (accessed August 18- 25, 2009)

National Sporting Goods Association. Sports Participation: http://www.nsga.org (accessed October 1 to November 20, 2009)

National Fishing Week: Planning your National Fishing Week Event. National Fishing Week Website. http://www.nationalfishingweek.co.uk/ (accessed September 20-25, 2009)

Ontario Ministry of Natural Resources. Take a Kid Fishing publication. http://www.mnr.gov.on.ca/en/Business/LetsFish/Publication/MNR_E001345P.html (accessed September 20-22, 2009)

Pat's boating in Canada: Helping boaters since 1996. Pat Drummond. Canadian Boating Statistic. http://boating.ncf.ca/ (accessed July 20-30, 2009)

Peter Kaminsky. The Top Ten World's Best Fishing Destinations. http://www.toptentopten.com/ (accessed October 20-22, 2009)

Responsive Management—Factors Related to Hunting and Fishing Participation among the Nation's Youth—http://www.responsivemanagement.com (accessed October 30 to November 12, 2009)

Trevor Corson. SuperChefblog. The Story of Sushi. http://www.superchefblog.com (accessed August 25-26, 2009)

The McNair Forty-acre Muskie (n.d) ThousandIslandslife.com http://www.thousandislandslife.com/BackIssues/Archive/tabid/393/articleType/ArticleView/articleId/170/The-MacNair-FortyAcre-Muskie.aspx (accessed July 25-26, 2009)

Transportation Safety Board of Canada (TSB). Statistical Summary Marine Occurrences (n. d.) http://www.tsb.gc.ca/ENG/stats/marine/2006/index.asp (accessed July 1-25, 2009)

Turtle Zen (n.d.) Weird Laws. http://www.turtlezen.com/weirdlaws.html (accessed July 15-July 18, 2009)

Wikipedia: The free encyclopedia. http://en.wikipedia.org/wiki/ (accessed July 1 to November 20, 2009)

Information was also used from the following print outlets

Ottawa Citizen, Ottawa SUN, Outdoor Canada, Outdoor Sportsman, Globe and Mail, National Geographic, ESPN Sports, Quebec Ministry of Tourism Lodging Brochure

Jeff Morrison

An avid sportsman, Jeff Morrison is a former *Ottawa Sun* columnist and a member of the Outdoor Writers of Canada. Currently, he has a blog under the moniker The Outdoors Guy for the *Ottawa Sun*, picking up where he left off with his column and encouraging local outdoor enthusiasts to share their thoughts. He has studied environmental science and fish and wildlife biology. When he realized that his passion for the outdoors could translate nicely into print and he could get paid for it, he set foot into the world of outdoor writing. When he's not writing, he's big-game hunting or chasing the ever-elusive world record brook trout from the wily waters of northern Quebec that he swears is waiting for him, taunting him at every cast.